A Pr

M000226517

HOW TO
WRITE A GRANT

Become a Grant Writing Unicorn

Meredith Noble

LEARNGRANTWRITING.ORG

Copyright © 2019 by SenecaWorks LLC

All rights reserved. This book or parts thereof may not be reproduced in any form, stored in any retrieval system, or transmitted in any form by any means—electronic, mechanical, photocopy, recording, or otherwise—without prior written permission of the publisher, expected as provided by U.S. copyright law. For permission requests, contact info@senworks.org.

Limit of Liability/Disclaimer of Warranty: The publisher and the author make no representations or warranties with respect to the accuracy or completeness of the contents of this work and specifically disclaim all warranties, including without limitation warranties of fitness for a particular purpose. The advice and strategies contained herein may not be suitable for every situation. The website (www.learngrantwriting.org) and the content provided herein are simply for educational purposes. This work is sold with the understanding that the publishered is not engaged in rendering legal, accounting or other professional services. If professional assistance is required, the services of a competent professional person should be sought.

Cover by Dejan Mijailovic
Book Design by Najdan Mancic

First Edition
ISBN 978-1-7333957-0-0
ISBN 978-1-7333957-1-7
ISBN 978-1-7333957-2-4

SenecaWorks LLC
721 Depot Drive, Anchorage AK 99501
www.learngrantwriting.org

DOWNLOAD THE AUDIOBOOK FREE!

Thank you for buying my book! To thank you, I would like to give you the audiobook version 100% free.

TO DOWNLOAD GO TO:

www.learngrantwriting.org/audiobook

CONTENTS

PART II : Questions Grant Writing Unicorns Ask Themselves

INTRODUCTION

Grant writers are by nature community change-makers. They are the 20% doing 80% of the work. They are quiet leaders, knowing how to build teams, forge community partnerships, and develop ideas into well-planned projects.

Grant writers put heart and soul into everything they do. They work on things that matter. They want to have an impact and better their communities.

Before grant writers become known for their craft, however, they started with an idea and plenty of ambition. Those that succeeded in taking their ideas and turning them into reality, learned the art of grant writing. Armed with this skill set, they were empowered to achieve their broader vision.

If this sounds like you, then you have come to the right place to get started.

What you have in your hands is a distillation of the most important information I know about grant writing. The book is structured with the first half answering the questions I am most frequently asked. The second half follows with the questions I wish you were asking.

The first chapter is by far the lengthiest. Do not let that overwhelm you! I wanted to put in a single chapter, the seven steps for writing grants. If you only read this one chapter (and adopt its practices), you will be leaps and bounds ahead of other aspiring grant writers.

We then dive into how to write a convincing narrative. Learning to write with persuasion and heart is a key ingredient to grant writing success. Many projects are worthy of funding but there is not enough grant funding for all. I show you how to make your proposal stand apart from the pack.

My favorite chapter is discussing how to find grants to go after. This is the part of the funding process that rewards creativity. Thinking "outside the box" will help you find funding opportunities others over-look. You will learn about an online grant database that will save you hundreds of hours researching grants and keeping track of them.

I then cover the most common issues that cause problems for grant writers, which is namely not hav-ing a funding strategy or sufficient project planning. This book will help you establish best practices for time management and learn how to focus on the grants with the best likelihood of success.

Armed with this information, you will be well on your way to becoming a grant writing unicorn!

PART I

Most Common Questions
Asked About Grant Writing

CHAPTER 1

HOW DO I WRITE A GRANT?

How do I become a grant writing unicorn? That is the most common question I am asked, well minus the unicorn part, but you are probably thinking it right? Grant writers are perceived to have super powers. They know how to get free money!

It is not quite that easy. There is no such thing as free money and grant writing is a lot of hard work. It is, however, an incredible skillset to have in your quiver and it is very learnable.

The trick is following consistent processes to stay on schedule and produce your best work. This chapter distills my best advice on how to write a grant in seven steps.

Step 1: Follow Your North Star (the Funding Guidelines).

Funding guidelines are instructions from the funder on how to apply. They usually include information on the grant program, eligibility, what the narrative requires, necessary attachments, etc.

You can download the funding guidelines from the funding agency website. Once downloaded, print them so you have a hard copy to mark up. You will catch nuances in the guidelines that, for some reason, are difficult to catch when reading on a computer.

Read the funding guidelines from beginning to end and then take a break. Go work on something else, stretch, pet your dog, whatever you do to maintain your energy. When you are done, come back to the guidelines and reread them carefully. I highlight keywords that are used repeatedly and specific instructions like font size requirements.

Be sure to locate the sections on what information the funder *wants in your grant narrative* and *the scoring criteria.*

Cannot find the scoring criteria? Not all funding guidelines tell you how the narrative will be evaluated and scored. If this is the case, pay extra attention to wording in the guidelines and the organization's website so you can align your narrative responses with those priorities.

Step 2: Prepare Your Narrative Skeleton.

Nothing is more intimidating than a blank page. To avoid feeling overwhelmed, I *always* prepare a 'narrative skeleton'. The skeleton is an outline for each section of the narrative and the scoring criteria.

Type into a blank document each narrative prompt and, if applicable, the scoring criteria. By doing this, you are preparing the exact headers and subheaders that the funding agency wants in your narrative.

Below is an example of a question pulled from a funding guideline that I typed into a grant narrative skeleton:

Rating Factor 1: Capacity of the Applicant

Subfactor 1.1.a Managerial and Technical Staff. *You must describe the project specific roles and responsibilities and knowledge/experience of the project director and all individual key staff in planning, managing, and implementing projects for which funding is requested. Experience pertaining to specific activities should be relevant, recent (in the last five years), and demonstrate that past projects were completed on or ahead of schedule.*

Scoring Criteria: *You describe the roles/responsibilities and the knowledge/experience of the project director and all individual key staff in planning, managing and implementing projects for which funding is being requested. Experience of all individual key staff is relevant, recent and successful.*

It may feel like a waste of time to be rewriting the application guidelines into your own text editor. The reason I encourage you to do this, however, is because it helps you start organizing your thoughts on how you are going to respond to each section.

Once the narrative skeleton is complete, start adding bullet points with ideas on how you want to respond to that question.

Do not start writing complete sentences! We just want bullet points for capturing ideas and questions, so you can see where you have gaps in information. From the example above, you may realize you need to collect specific project examples from key team members on their recent and relevant experience delivering projects on schedule.

Once you have a complete narrative skeleton with bullet points, you will have a robust understanding of what is needed to prepare the proposal.

Even then, we still do not start writing! The next step is hosting an official grant kick-off meeting.

Step 3: Host an Outstanding Kick-Off Meeting.

A kick-off meeting is where we gather everyone involved in the project to plan for the grant preparation process. The amount of help you receive during the grant writing process is directly correlated to the success of your kick-off meeting.

I will often bring cookies or provide lunch to express my gratitude to the group for giving their time to help me prepare an application. If people feel appreciated and inspired by you, they will make your requests a priority.

Prepare an agenda beforehand and email it one day in advance. Pictured here is an example of a meeting agenda. You can also download a free template at **www.learngrantwriting.org/free-grant-writing-resources.**

SAMPLE MEETING AGENDA

Date: *Monday, December 3, 2020*

Time: *9:30—10:15 AM*

Host: *Your Name Goes Here*

Attendees: *Guest Names Here*

RE: *Kick Off Meeting for <Grant Name> Application*

Topic

Introductions:

Brief intros for everyone in attendance.

Objective: To agree on how to best share responsibilities of the <grant name here> application.

Project Overview:

» Confirm agreement on project scope being pursued for funding.

Questions:

» Add your specific questions here that you gathered while preparing the grant narrative skeleton.

» What is a grant narrative skeleton?
Learn how to create one here:
**https://www.learngrantwriting.org/
narrative-writing-training-course**

Narrative/Attachment Requirements (EXAMPLE):

» Narrative—Lisa lead, Meredith support

» SF-424 Form—Lisa

» HUD-2880—Lisa

» HUD-4125 Implementation
Schedule—Meredith

» HUD -4123 Cost Summary—Meredith

» Citizen Participation Resolution—Lisa
Prepares. Andrea Gets Passed.

Review Narrative Skeleton:

Provide a copy of your grant narrative skeleton
and review it quickly with the team. Identify who
will contribute what information. For example,
when you get to the project team section of the
narrative, you may identify that everyone on the
team needs to provide their resumes.

Schedule:

See below.

Wrap Up:

Agree on next meeting date and time.

SAMPLE SCHEDULE

Mon	Tues	Wed	Thurs	Fri
3 Kick Off Meeting	4 Receive Info Requested	5 Draft resolution to submit grant	6 Request letters of support	7 Draft #1 budget form
10 Draft #1 narrative due	11 Team meeting	12	13 Pass Resolution	14
17 Draft #2 narrative due	18 Team meeting	19 Letters of Support Due	20 Finalize budget form	21 Draft #3 narrative due

24	25	26	26	28
	Team edits to narrative due	Draft #4 narrative due	Draft #4 narrative due	Finalize application for review
31	1	2	3	4
Independent review	Finalize. Submit grant!	Grant due date		

My agenda template includes names of attendees, date, time and subject. I will start off with introductions if needed. I will then provide a copy of the narrative skeleton. I run through it quickly asking where I can get information that I need to prepare the application. Team members often come up with ideas for additional information or resources to reference when they can see the narrative skeleton themselves.

I close out the meeting by discussing the grant development schedule. It is best to learn now if someone will be unavailable because of vacation or other work obligations. Even if you carry 99% of the responsibility for completing the grant application, it is still important to establish a schedule with dead-lines for your own accountability.

Following the meeting, send out an email summarizing action items and a calendar invite for the next progress meeting. I try to schedule progress meetings to last no longer than 30-40 minutes. Shorter meetings help attendees feel refreshed enough to complete their action items immediately.

Step 4: Finalize the Grant Budget.

I am assuming you have at least a rough cost estimate for your project. In a perfect world, project budgets would be nearly complete before starting an application, but it never seems to work out that way.

However, finalizing your budget is now your top priority! The project budget impacts other parts of your application and progress will be impeded if it is not finalized.

For instance, if a grant requires 50% of the project cost to be funded by the applicant, it is impossible to calculate your cost-share without knowing the total project cost. An applicant's cost share commitment must be documented in a formal resolution or letter from someone authorized in your organization to do so. It can be a time consuming and formal process to get a resolution passed.

Grant applications often require a budget narrative to describe how you developed a reasonable cost estimate. It is challenging to write a budget narrative without a complete budget!

Most narratives also require an implementation plan and description on the benefits of the project. Does your budget allow you to impact the lives of 20 homeless Veterans or 200? Will you renovate four low-income housing units or 14?

I am guessing the last few paragraphs were pretty overwhelming! Before you give up, know that none of that will be an issue for you if you have a finalized project budget. As such, I cannot emphasize enough the importance of finishing your budget as soon as possible.

Check out Chapter 10 for a detailed description on how to prepare a project budget and download your free copy of our grant budget template at ***www.learngrantwriting.org/free-grant-writing-resources.***

Step 5: Write Your Narrative Fast and Furiously.

A narrative is a written description about your project, the problem it solves, and why it should be funded.

The exact nature of your narrative will vary depending on the requirements of each funding agency. Sometimes, a private foundation will ask for a letter of inquiry first. This is usually a two page letter summarizing your proposal. If the funder likes your proposal, you will be invited to submit a full application. Other times, a grant narrative is going to be fifteen pages of single-spaced writing with other lengthy and technical attachments.

Your grant narrative should always be customized for the grant for which you are applying. You can certainly recycle text from previous applications, but it must be intentionally reworked to fit the grant guidelines.

» **Prepare your first draft as fast as possible.** I want your first draft of the narrative completed in no more than 8-10 business days from when you started.

It is tempting to leave your narrative to track down information. At all costs, avoid doing this! Often the information you seek gets deleted in later drafts anyway, and it costs you too much time and energy to refocus.

For example, if I write about who benefits from the project, it is tempting to stop mid-sentence to look up supporting data. Instead I will write a sentence like this: "XX% of the project beneficiaries are low to moderate income." Later on I will look up the exact statistic.

Consider writing your grant narrative backwards. The harder sections are usually towards the end of your grant narrative and include topics like budgeting, project feasibility, etc. Working through the complex portions of the application first makes it easier to write the beginning sections, which are typically broader strokes.

Tip: *Dreading the idea of writing a long narrative? Here is a time saving hack for you! Record yourself talking slowly and clearly about each section of the narrative. Use your grant narrative skeleton developed in Step 2 to guide your recording. Then use any number of online resources to convert your audio file into text. The text file will not capture punctuation, but it is much easier to edit than writing your first draft from scratch. This method can save hours of writing!*

» **Stay accountable to writing deadlines by collaborating with someone else.** It is invaluable to find someone that will accept your progress writing a grant narrative. Your "accountability buddy" does not need to read your earliest, messiest versions of the narrative, but by having them accept your drafts, it keeps you accountable to writing deadlines. Send your progress every 2-3 days to inspire working quickly.

Identify who this person will be during the grant kick-off meeting. Ideally, it is someone within your organization. If you do not have someone in your organization to collaborate with, ask a friend or other working professional that you can repay the favor later.

When I was just starting my business, I hired my sister to edit my grant narratives. She named her price by putting something she wanted in my Amazon cart, and I was happy to pay for it because of the mistakes that she caught. When we spend a lot of time working on a narrative, we become blind to silly mistakes. Prevent errors and write faster by promising someone your grant writing progress.

» **Edit, edit, and edit some more.** After you complete your first draft of the narrative, I want *at least* four more versions. Save a new version after every major edit, because sometimes you will have deleted something that you want to resurrect. Great writing is concise and clear. The only way you get to that level of brevity is to continually iterate. On complex grants, I will have as many as 15 different narrative drafts!

 Tip: *Instead of Microsoft Word, try using Google Docs because Google Docs automatically keeps track of your version history.*

Step 6: Manage Your Attention and Focus.

The key to successful grant writing is setting yourself up with the right conditions to focus.

» **Download files from your email inbox to a project folder immediately.** Nothing compromises your productivity more than looking for information and getting sidetracked.

Touch an email once. If you receive an attachment or email with useful information in it, download it immediately and put it in your project folder. This way, you can access that information without getting distracted by opening your inbox. This also is important for those times when you may be working remotely or in a meeting with limited internet access. Having a local copy of these documents will allow you to access them regardless of Internet connectivity.

» **Schedule your narrative writing for the morning.** If your workplace has morning meetings, consider asking they be moved to the afternoon so you can use your most focused hours of the day writing.

I try to not check my email until I have completed the most important priority from my day. When I am grant writing, that means writing some substantial portion of the narrative first before doing anything else.

» **Set a timer to complete bite size pieces of your application.** Most people thrive under a little pressure created by deadlines. I do not want you to actually procrastinate, but we can recreate that sense of urgency by having several mini deadlines.

I strive to work in 90-minute blocks with a full hour of rest in between. In that hour, I take a walk, stretch, eat healthy food, catch up with friends, take a nap, etc. Whatever you do, leave your computer and stop thinking about the grant. It is imperative to keep your energy and creativity high, so you can do your best work when you sit down to write.

A lot of times, if I am struggling to make progress, I will break those blocks down into even smaller chunks. I will set a timer for 20—40 minutes, which is short enough I can pledge to be distraction free.

» **If you cannot access a state of deep work in your office, find somewhere else to go.** The average office employee is distracted or interrupted every ten minutes. It can take 25 minutes to refocus! There is no way to be an effective grant writer with that level of distraction.

Consider going to your public library, a co-working office, or even a friend's house. Do not assume there is no way your boss will let you work somewhere else. Most people understand the challenge of staying focused and distraction free and are willing to accommodate.

» **Use Post-Its to capture random to-do thoughts while you are writing.** Nobody likes to suffer, but muscling through a grant narrative can feel painful! Your brain is going to try to sabotage your progress by attacking you with thoughts of all of the things you need to do.

To gain control of your mind, write down each of these tasks on a Post-It. Then place each Post-It on a calendar next to your desk to establish what day you will take care of it. I try to stack a bunch of small tasks into my "loose ends day," which I will save for an afternoon when I can take care of them in bulk.

By writing down every random task that pops into your mind, you allow yourself to forget about it and move on with your narrative without fearing you will forget the task. This practice also helps you to be practical about managing your time. Chances are, the task is not something that actually needs to be dealt with right now. Prioritize your narrative as it requires the most time and mental bandwidth.

With healthy time management practices in place, you will complete your grant application package stress-free and on or ahead of schedule. Now comes the final step!

Step 7: Have an Independent Review of Your Entire Application.

Part of what makes grants so intimidating is the number of moving parts. You have the narrative, several attachments, the application submittal process, and more. Even if you are impeccably well organized, it can be easy to make a mistake.

To prevent this, plan to have someone provide an independent review of your entire application. This person needs to be different from whoever helped you with editing the narrative. They need to bring a completely fresh set of eyes to the application.

Turn in your application *at least one day early,* but preferably two. Most people are not managing their time well and submit their application at the very last minute. Avoid burnout, unnecessary stress, and embarrassing mistakes by submitting your grant early.

You now know the seven steps to write a grant! The trick to being a grant writing unicorn is simply following the funding guidelines to a tee, being the best project manager you can be, and learning to manage your focus. Mastering those principles will make you an unstoppable force.

ACTION YOU CAN TAKE RIGHT NOW

✓ Develop a grant kick-off meeting agenda template that you can reuse over and over.

✓ Download your free budget spreadsheet template and finalize your cost estimate. It takes time to develop a budget, so jump in now!

✓ Start practicing good energy management habits: block time for deep work, take energizing breaks, and batch smaller tasks together to save time.

CHAPTER 2

HOW DID YOU LEARN GRANT WRITING?

I earned grant writing the way most of us learn: I climbed into the driver's seat and gave it a go. Parallel parking used to require a lot of brainpower. Now I can whip into any parking spot without thinking twice.

Writing grants is the same. Something that used to take me six weeks, I can now do in two. I went from having a deathly fear of grant budgets to being able to prepare one for any topic.

Getting to that point, however, did not come easy. (Hence my inspiration to save you time learning everything the hard way!)

Here is the story of how I learned grant writing:

I graduated from college in the midst of the economic recession. Jobs were far from abundant. I did informational interviews with anyone that would agree to it.

I wanted to get into the engineering profession, but I had graduated with a marketing degree. I made a point of arranging a meeting with any engineering or architecture firm that would meet. I wanted to learn more about their business and find ways I could help.

Three to six months later, many of those firms reached out for help with their writing and graphic design needs. One of the projects I was hired for was preparing a transportation improvement grant.

I loved it! I thrived in the triangle between technical engineers, the funding agency, and the client.

A few months later, the firm offered me a full-time job as a grant writer. It did not take long for project managers in the company to ask for my help in obtaining funding for their clients.

I remember my first big project vividly. It was helping get a tribal clinic funded. The tribe had tried unsuccessfully for ten years. Even worse, they had received funding at one point, but they had to give it back because they did not own the property where the clinic would go.

I was brought on to figure out what kind of funding the tribe should pursue. The funding research process took me several weeks. (I can now complete the same process in a day, and I will show you how in Chapter 4.)

I worked hard to prepare and submit that first grant application. Then I spent several months agonizing over what I would do if it was not successful. I convinced myself that if it was not funded, I would quit my job. I feared failure, for it would be proof that I did not know what I was doing.

We are likely here today because that grant was successful, and I did not irrationally quit! I then went on to help the tribe secure the $4 million needed to fully fund the clinic. When the clinic was built, I hugged the building, gave my team members high-fives, and cried tears of joy.

I was learning everything on the job as I went. Since this position was new, I did not have anyone to mentor me. I was inexperienced and adopted the mantra, "fake it 'till you make it."

After my first year, our company of 150 people was acquired by a multi-national firm with 15,000 employees. Word spread about my work.

I was called upon to help fund water treatment plants, transportation infrastructure, broadband, stormwater mitigation, skateparks, you name it!

Things were going well, but I often felt out of my league and overwhelmed. I quickly discovered that writing a grant was not the hard part! It was figuring out the steps that come before that, like what grants existed, how to decide which ones to pursue, and piecing together multiple funding streams.

At some point, I felt like I had been winging it long enough, and I wanted continuing education to improve my skills. I looked at a number of grant workshops and trainings. They were expensive and too generalized. There were no options for online learning.

I never found a course in which I had enough confidence to ask my company to pay for, so I went back to the way I always did it, teaching myself, and learning on the go. Through a fair amount of failures and lessons learned the hard way, I figured it out!

What emerged is my own unique way of doing things. I am actually not that organized, so I built processes around that weakness to be more detail oriented. Many of those tips are discussed in Chapter 6.

Probably my most unique skill set is knowing how to put together a roadmap for getting projects funded. I will show you how in Chapter 11 and 12.

I made plenty of mistakes learning how to be a grant writer. I celebrate those failures and share them openly. Here is one particularly traumatic failure to give you an idea:

I was hired as a support grant writer to prepare an application for a hydroelectric project. Immediately, I had reservations about the applicant being eligible.

I tried to contact the funding agency representatives listed in the funding guidelines. I called every phone number and sent a message to every email address I could find, and I almost never got through to anyone. When I did, I would not get a straight answer as to whether the applicant was eligible or not. I was sent complex legal jargon that made my head spin.

I persisted and eventually got in writing that the applicant was eligible to apply. I still felt wary about it, but we were getting closer to the grant deadline every day. No one else on the project team was sharing my reservations about being eligible, so I told myself to stop overreacting.

A few days before the grant was due, I went mountain biking. I was having a lot of trouble riding my bike that day. I kept crashing! Then I crashed one time too many times and broke my collarbone. It was the first bone I had ever broken.

I had surgery right away, but all I could think about was finishing the grant. I worked through the pain and discomfort, and turned in a beautiful proposal on the deadline, which was also my birthday.

A few months later, we found out the application was not eligible and that the entire effort was a waste of time and money. This was crushing for a number of reasons. Mostly, I was frustrated with myself for dismissing my concerns about eligibility.

I learned a lot from the experience.

For one, I learned that as an applicant, you must be 100% positive that your project is eligible for funding before spending hours preparing an application.

Secondly, I learned to trust my intuition. Since then, I have the confidence to stop a project if necessary.

Lastly, I learned the importance of maintaining your health when grant writing.

 Tip: *This profession makes you feel like you are constantly sprinting towards deadlines, but grant writing is actually an endurance sport. Thus, take care of yourself mentally and physically, and you will succeed.*

People think grant writers have super powers, but as you can tell from my story, we are all human. We never finish learning how to be grant writers. It is a field that is always changing, and experience provides new learning outcomes on every grant. Even grants I write today provide me with new insights and experience.

I hope that my story gives you confidence that you can do this. If I can learn, you can too!

CHAPTER 3

HOW DO YOU WRITE A CONVINCING NARRATIVE?

This excerpt is from a grant application to the U.S. Department of Environmental Protection Agency for brownfield redevelopment grant funding:

> *"Because Anchorage grew so fast with the construction of the Trans-Alaska Pipeline, the area lacked land use policies and enforcement resources. When oil prices dropped in 1986-88 it caused the 'Great Alaskan Recession' where nearly one in ten jobs were lost. Businesses folded and abandoned their properties and to this day, many remain vacant. Known and suspected contamination on these sites has impeded*

their redevelopment and depressed proper-
ty values…The former 4th Avenue Theater in
Downtown is a cherished historical icon but
rapidly deteriorating. It has numerous code
deficiencies, asbestos, and a petroleum re-
lease from an underground storage tank.
Many downtown businesses have relocat-
ed to midtown leaving brownfields in their
wake."

Did that catch your attention? Do things seem dire? Evidently, it did for the funding agency too because the applicant was funded.

I will never forget when a funding agency representative told me I needed to use the word catastrophic more. *Catastrophic.* The word felt a little extreme and theatrical, but I learned what she meant.

I needed to establish that the project was in dire need of funding. I needed to establish urgency for the project and why it could not wait another year for funding.

Tip: *Remember, we are not writing just to present facts. We are writing to persuade.*

Move your reader. Tell them stories that help them understand the bigger context for why your project matters. Do not just explain *what* you are going to do, show them *why.*

Here is a breakdown of my top seven suggestions for writing convincingly:

STEP 1: Convince yourself to your very core why the project is important.

You have to genuinely believe in it, so much so that you describe it with passion when you speak with friends and family.

Grant writing is like being in sales. It is hard to sell something if you do not believe in it. I only take on projects that I personally find interesting and important—I have to believe in them. You should do the same. Life is too short to work on projects that do not speak to our hearts.

STEP 2: Be clear about what problem you are solving.

I see a lot of projects try to get funded because it is "a good idea." Ideas are plentiful. Funding organizations want their grant investments to *solve real problems* and create positive change.

I helped an art project mature from idea to implementation and secure early-stage funding. I described the problem we were solving in grant narratives, but it was my wording—not owned by the team. Project leaders would not think of their idea as solving a problem, and this ultimately led me to leave the team because of the uphill battle that created in securing larger grants.

STEP 3: Know your WHY arguments.

Here are some questions to ask yourself when trying to define your best arguments for *why your project matters*:

» **Why does this project matter to your community?** How are you making your community stronger?

» **What other things can happen by developing this project?** Can other investments be made because funding is freed up? Is there a domino effect; if this project happens, will two or three others also fall into place?

» **What happens if this project is not funded?**

» **What are the regional implications?** Does your project transcend your organization's boundaries to affect others?

Here is an example: for several years, salmon were not returning to the Yukon River in Alaska and fishing was prohibited. Alaska Native communities that rely on salmon harvest for their food needs were heavily impacted. Household finances were strained by the need to fly untraditional foods out to their rural communities. A generation of young people never learned how to pre-serve salmon from their elders.

The salmon run returned, and the local village wanted to do something about the knowledge that was lost. The project became a joint effort between the community's elders and young people to build a smoke-house for drying and preserving salmon.

In the grant narratives, we did not just focus on the youth that would benefit. We talked about the lifelong, multigenerational effects on culture when knowledge sharing is broken. We pledged to share our learnings with others in the region, so that other tribes could mimic the project. Our funding efforts were successful because we focused on why the project mattered in a larger context.

STEP 4: Leverage your grants like dominoes.

Funders want their dollars to go as far as possible. You establish urgency by showing that additional funding can be leveraged *if this grant is awarded.* Paint a picture in your narrative of grant funding you have pursued or will pursue to demonstrate the relationship between funding sources.

> *For example, I did an electric bus grant application. We drove home the urgency of funding the project by talking about a public bond that had been approved, the first transit bond in years. We pointed out that that funding would not be available after the next year because the funds would be spent. That meant that we needed the grant award this year, or we would not have match funding from the bond. This technique helps establish urgency.*

STEP 5: Present your project team confidently and prove why they are the best.

Funders know that projects will be successful because of the people behind them. You must demonstrate throughout the grant application that you have a capable team with relevant experience.

Spend time thinking about why your team has exceptional leaders to execute the project plan and relay that reasoning in your narrative.

When I was first learning grant writing, I found a grant writer in Seattle who had successfully secured a career's worth of research grants in Antarctica. I bribed him with a beer to teach me his ways! The one thing that sticks with me to this day was his emphasis on assembling the *best* team you can. Strong teams win projects. This usually means putting together unlikely combinations of people and stakeholders.

You do not have to make do with the staff in your organization. Think beyond your organization's boundaries. Who can you partner with to strengthen the areas in which you are weaker? If you do not have strong financial management capacity in-house, partner with an accountant. If you are not experienced in measuring program impact, partner with someone that does.

Many times, people get hung up on sharing funding with other organizations. Remember, receiving

60% of the grant is better than no grant! Plus, partnerships drastically increase your odds of success because they show broad support.

STEP 6: Be convincing with a great plan for making the project happen.

Scope of work, implementation plan, work plan— whatever you want to call it, it is where you convince the grant reviewer that you have a realistic plan for making the project happen.

Too often, I see grant narratives that basically say they will figure it out once they are funded. While that may be true to a degree, we do not want it to come across that way to the grant reviewer. They want to know that you have thought through the project carefully and are ready to implement immediately.

Chances are good you are not leading the project you are describing in your narrative. However, more often than not, you will get stuck writing the scope of work! You may feel totally unqualified to do this, but you have to jump in and take ownership.

It can be stressful and overwhelming to prepare a technical scope of work. The painless way for doing this is to ask for bullet points from the technical staff or person responsible for implementing the project. This is less overwhelming for them and they can typically drop that information into an email.

You can also meet with the technical person and audio record their responses to the grant narrative questions you have. Smartphones have a voice recording application by default. If you want, you can then convert the audio file to text through any number of online services, and you have a good start!

Massage the information provided to you into the grant narrative to the best of your ability. When you are done, take the narrative back to your technical person and ask them to edit it. It works like a charm! Repeat as necessary.

Remember, if you cannot distill the scope of work into something easy enough for you to understand, then your grant reviewer will not understand it either.

STEP 7: Answer the narrative questions exactly.

You are convincing when you answer the narrative prompts directly and clearly. You do not usually need to regurgitate text from elsewhere in the application; you can reference those sections.

Often, a section of a narrative will have multiple questions. How do you make sure you are responding to all parts? I handle this by writing a starting sentence for each question in my response and bolding and italicizing it. By making it effortless to find the answer, I help the grant reviewer spot my response to each of the questions.

Below is an example of a question from a Small Business Innovation Research grant:

The Market Opportunity—Describe the market and addressable market for the innovation. Discuss the business economics and market drivers in the target industry. How has the market opportunity been validated? Describe your customers and your basic go to market strategy to achieve the market opportunity. Describe the competition. How do you expect the competitive landscape may change by the time your product/service enters the market? What are the key risks in bringing your innovation to market? Describe your commercialization approach. Discuss the potential economic benefits associated with your innovation, and provide estimates of the revenue potential, detailing your underlying assumptions. Describe the resources you expect will be needed to implement your commercialization approach.

If that seems like a hardcore section to respond to, you are correct! It was intimidating to write! It would be easy to only answer about half of this. I had to be intentional to make sure we responded to every question.

In my early grant narrative drafts, I had a paragraph for each question. Below is an abbreviated version to give you an idea of what the final product looked like:

Addressable Market. *Nationally there are 700,000+ US family ranches that fit the pasture-raised ranch profile, primarily across the US West.*

Business Economics/Market Drivers: *Companies that are thriving today are those that recognize how the convergence of technology and changing consumer preferences affect business. Nielsen's Global Sustainability Report in 2015 found that 69% of global consumers pay more for organic/natural foods that are sustainably sourced (Nielsen, 2015). When coupled specifically with the growing body of evidence that grass fed and pasture raised beef can have up to half the fat and cholesterol of lot-raised beef, demand for proven sources of sustainable beef will continue to increase in coming years (Yeager, 2015).*

Market Validation: *The market opportunity has been validated by early adoption from local Wyoming ranches to participate in pilot tests, extensive press coverage, and strong interest from venture-capital investors.*

The bottom line is that you want to make it excessively clear where you response is to each of the funder's questions.

By following these seven tips, you are well on your way to writing a convincing narrative! Use your best creative and analytical thinking skills to develop persuasive arguments. Do not just state the facts. Persuade the funder that your project is more deserving of funding than other worthy projects.

ACTION YOU CAN TAKE RIGHT NOW

✓ Write down in a few sentences why you work with the organization you do and why the project personally matters to you.

✓ Type up a one paragraph project description. Specify the problem you are solving.

✓ Add in bullet points for why the project matters to your beneficiaries and the community at large.

✓ Brainstorm other grants and funding sources you can leverage against each other.

✓ Audit the strengths and weaknesses of your team. Determine if you need to find additional partners to form an unbeatable team.

CHAPTER 4

HOW DO YOU FIND GRANTS TO GO AFTER?

Instrumentl.com. My work here is done! Okay, not quite, but whenever I want to offer advice of immediate value, I send people to Instrumentl.com—a fabulous online grant database.

This relatively new company was started by Angela Braren, Katharine Corriveau, and Gauri Manglik who spent their careers in the nonprofit sector. They also experienced frustration in figuring out what grants exist, and luckily for us, they decided to do something about it!

Years ago when I was creating a video for my online class on how to research funding, I was doing it the way I have always done it—searching through

Google. I then accidentally stumbled upon Instrumentl.

I had to stop filming and completely rethink my approach to funding research. I signed up for a free two-week trial and fell in love with the service. Grant research used to take me 10-20 hours, and now I can do it 1-2 hours! It is incredible.

You can also hire expert grant writers through Instrumentl. If your organization can afford to hire an extra grant writer to help you, it is worth it. I have hired grant writers for my company, SenecaWorks, numerous times through the platform to expand my internal team for specific grant projects.

If you want a full debrief on how I use this tool, it is discussed in my online grant writing class and on our YouTube channel. To see first-hand what this powerful tool can do, set up a free trial and check it out for yourself at **www.instrumentl.com**.

You can also use a search engine like Google to research project funding. I have tried almost every other database that exists, including having an intern one summer try to create one! Nothing I have found beats the combination of using Instrumentl with basic online searching.

Here is what you need to know as you start researching:

Types of Funding. There are several different categories of funding for you to consider. There are federal grants and low interest loans that are available nationwide. State grants, as the name implies, are specific funding opportunities to your state. Local grants can come from your local government or community organizations. Private foundations range in size from national, regional, and local.

Foundations generally make awards to nonprofit organizations that have 501(c)3 status with the Internal Revenue Service. If you are not a nonprofit, it is worth finding one you can partner with to access additional streams of funding.

Think Creatively. My success in finding funding comes from thinking about projects creatively. For example, if you search "grants for skateparks", you will find information on the Tony Hawk Foundation. You will not see a lot more than that because Tony Hawk takes up all top search results. The maximum you can apply for from the Tony Hawk Foundation is $25,000. Skateparks are anywhere from $300,000 to $4,000,000+.

When I was trying to figure out how to get a skatepark funded in Massachusetts, I came at it from every angle imaginable:

» **Adjacent Land Uses.** Next to the skatepark was a large senior housing complex. Research shows that loneliness is one of the main contributors to poor health in seniors. I explored grant opportunities to make seniors feel welcome spending time at the skatepark. Not only does this give them a lively show, it helps detract from unwanted behaviors often associated with skateparks. I found a grant for a shaded seating structure from a national dermatology association. Perfect!

» **Community Health.** I researched how the project improves health outcomes, particularly in combating obesity in youth. Fewer youth are participating in organized sport teams and are instead choosing 'individual' sports like biking and skateboarding. To make our case here, I looked at how many low to moderate income youth lived within walking or skating distance of the proposed skatepark. I did not end up finding anything I liked enough to recommend, but this gives you an idea of my thought process even if it was a dead end.

» **Environmental Benefit.** One of the biggest expenses for a skate park is the site work. I brainstormed if the parking lot could have permeable pavement (meaning stormwater can flow through it and not runoff with pollutants). I was curious what other low-impact development techniques could be applied to the site to protect the lake nearby from stormwater pollution. Educational signage could be put up at the skatepark to teach the kids (and adults!) about stormwater. I found a number of environmental and water protection grants that could fund education and site development work.

» **Community Identity.** The community has a rich history in glass blowing. I researched ways we could incorporate art grants into the skatepark, perhaps making rideable art pieces. It would give the skatepark local flair and involve a sector of the community that would not naturally collaborate with skateboarders. I found several promising art grants.

» **Brownfield Redevelopment.** Brownfields are properties that are complicated to redevelop as they are contaminated or perceived to be contaminated. Often a skatepark can be an excellent site remediation tool, because the cement surface can cap the contaminated soils to prevent further leaching into groundwater. Sounds gross I know, but there is funding for this!

The takeaway from the example above is to think about your project in smaller "bite-size" elements. It sometimes helps to look at your budget to see how certain line items could be funded separately.

My recommendation? Marry ***Instrumentl.com*** with Google searching and local knowledge. As much as I love Instrumentl, I have found that it does not always find everything. The tool gets better every day, but you can not replace local knowledge on programs that are unique to your state and region. Here are additional steps you can take to learn about more opportunities.

Get involved with your community. I am wrapping up a project right now for a senior housing development. Instrumentl did not show funding from the Alaska Housing Finance Corporation, but this is our best funding opportunity for low-interest loans and grants. I knew about it by being a part of the community and generally knowing what is available locally.

As you enter the world of grant writing, you will quickly pick up on the big players that give through philanthropy and private foundations. You can also start to learn about unique regional opportunities available to you by searching the websites of state departments.

Talk to other grant writers. Reach out to organizations that successfully secure grant funding and learn from them. Those that take our online grant writing courses get access to an online community that operates a lot like Facebook. We provide continued access even after you graduate from the program for the ongoing benefit of collaborating with other grant writing unicorns.

Put all of your grant findings in one place for easy review. In a spreadsheet, list all of the funding opportunities you are considering. It is easier to assess your findings against each other when they are listed in one place. The spreadsheet we use has the following columns:

- » **Funding Agency**
- » **Funding Program Name**
- » **What the Program Funds**
- » **Eligibility**
- » **Amount of Funding Available and Match Requirements**
- » **Deadline**
- » **Where to Learn More**

You can download a free matrix spreadsheet at **www.learngrantwriting.org/free-grant-writing-resources.**

In the grant research process, I usually find at least 15 different sources. These opportunities do not have equal likelihood of success, nor do they represent the same return on investment. The part that requires tact and thoughtfulness is getting that list of 15-20 funding sources down to a select few actually worth pursuing. However, that is a topic for Chapter 11!

ACTION YOU CAN TAKE RIGHT NOW

✓ Make a list of out-of-the-box search terms for researching grant funding.

✓ Visit our LearnGrantWriting YouTube channel to watch a video on searching grant opportunities on Instrumentl.

✓ Set up a free trial with Instrumentl.
   com. If you end up buying a
   subscription, use discount code
   mnoble0193 for $75 off.

✓ Download your free funding matrix
   spreadsheet to keep track of your grant
   findings at **www.learngrantwriting.org/
   free-grant-writing-resources.**

CHAPTER 5

I JUST LEARNED ABOUT {GRANT NAME}, BUT IT IS DUE IN {IN-SANELY SHORT TIMEFRAME}. SHOULD I GO AFTER IT?

The answer is no.

"But this is the PERFECT grant for us!"

Here is the deal: if you are only learning about a grant once the announcement has come out, you are too late. You do not have the time to properly examine if it is a good fit. Your judgment is now blurry because you want the signs to say "go for it!"

Even if you follow my rules of contacting the funding agency to gauge if the program is a good fit for your project and organization, the funder can lead you astray. Once an announcement is out, many funders will encourage you to apply because it makes their programs look better if they are competitive. Another issue often becomes that a funding agency representative cannot talk to you about your project once grant announcements have been made.

Remember, I do not come up with this advice out of nowhere. It is because I learned the lesson the hard way—a few times. Even when you know better, you can fall into the trap of thinking "this one grant is the exception to the rule, and I am going to go for it!"

I once dropped everything to help a local nonprofit pursue a national arts grant. It seemed like the perfect fit, and they desperately needed the funding. The application was pretty easy, so I agreed to prepare the application with just a few days notice.

I imagine you can guess what happened. The application was not successful. It also took me forever to figure this out because, in my haste to apply, I had misspelled the email for our main point of contact. Insert face palm emoji here.

I later figured out that only 1-2% of applicants were successful. Generally, my rule of thumb is to not apply for grants with less than a 20% chance of getting funded[1]. If I had taken the time to properly research the grant program, I would have learned how competitive it was and never applied.

Another common sentiment I hear is that, **"It is a simple application and will not take long to prepare."** Do not be fooled into thinking a two-page application will not take time. In fact, the shorter the application, the more your word choice matters, and that requires more editing time.

If you drop everything to spend a week preparing an application that has low odds of success, you can easily waste a full 30-60 hours of work on nothing. Even if it was "just a day"—that is a day you are not getting back!

What if you put that time into developing your project further and putting together a proper funding strategy? (A funding strategy is a roadmap for

---

[1] www.learngrantwriting.org/blog/must-do-math-before-writing-a-grant

knowing what grants to pursue and when. We show you how to develop one in Chapters 11 and 12.)

"My boss insists I apply. I do not have a choice." Okay, first of all, you do have a choice. A boss never threatens you to write the grant *or else.* (And if that is the case, you should probably find a new job!) Their demand is coming from wanting that grant resource and trusting you to get it done.

To counteract these demands, you must find your voice and paint your case with facts. Here are three tests you can use to quickly gauge if a grant is worth precious organization resources:

> **Test #1: What is the likelihood of getting funded?** You calculate this by dividing the total number of applicants by the number of awards made. You will do this for the previous year's program.
>
> Many times, you can not figure out how many applicants applied. You will have to contact the funding agency and ask. This is

an easy question to open up communication with the funding agency representative.

I target a ratio that is no less than 20%. If there are 100 applicants and 24 of those are funded, that means we have a 24% chance of getting funded. I am good with those odds. I will sometimes dip down into the 13-15% range, but I must have strong reasons for doing so.

Test #2: Does the funding agency support projects or organizations like yours? Often, when you are feeling pressured to hurry and apply, it is because someone is interpreting text on the project website as the "perfect fit." The language used on a funder's website does not always reflect their current giving priorities.

If you are applying for private foundation funding, you can access their giving history by reviewing their 990 forms filed with the Internal Revenue Service. These are gold mines of good information!

Tip: *Locate 990 forms for free through the Foundation Center or your Instrumentl.com subscription.*

If the funding program says it funds fighting obesity, saving the polar bears, and art and culture, look at their 990 form to confirm if this is true. Perhaps then you see that they actually only fund arts and culture projects, so do not bother with your grant request to save the polar bears!

Test #3: What is the true cost of grant preparation? Even simple applications have a cost for preparation. Take your hourly rate and add 20-30% for your benefits (like healthcare, retirement savings, insurance, etc.). Multiply that by the number of hours you would spend on this project. Do the same for anyone else involved.

We think our time is free, but it is not. It is good to be clear on what those costs are, so you use the precious resource of time wisely.

Confirm that the grant award is worth more than the time it takes to apply.

It can be hard to advocate for not pursuing a grant, but be confident with your intuition, even if you are a new grant writer. Early in my career, I went head to head with an engineer that wanted to pursue wastewater treatment funding for a community that had no chance of getting awarded. This community had the lowest service fees state-wide for providing wastewater services.

The project they were trying to get funded was frankly just a routine maintenance improvement. The City did not need a grant; they needed to raise their rates. The engineer fought me on this and said, "It earns us goodwill if we show the community we tried".

I explained my logic, and we agreed it was a waste of time to prepare the application. I have done this countless times since then when it does not make sense to apply.

Sometimes, a grant looks like a great fit, but once you get into the thick of it, you realize some fatal flaw. Do not try to hide it. If you see it, the funder will too.

If you do not believe in your heart that you have a good chance at winning the grant, do not waste your time!

 Tip: *Grants are too much work to not focus exclusively on those providing the best chance of winning.*

Why This Matters. Crash preparation of grant applications is a recipe for burnout. Grant writing is a lot like the role that marketing coordinators have in professional consulting companies. The average burnout is three years, and it is because they are always on deadlines.

If you want to be in the game for the long run, you have to intentionally avoid burnout. Otherwise, you will never want to write another grant again. That is what happened to me! (I have since recovered and continue to enjoy grant writing.)

In addition, you can tarnish your reputation if you always rush things and beg favors from people so that you can make a grant deadline. It is unprofessional to ask for last-minute letters of support or rush a resolution from your council or board of directors. We all need favors from time to time, but ask for them wisely.

There are exceptions to the rule, but you must take responsibility for a negative outcome if you choose to apply. Have I ever dropped everything to apply for a grant with an impossibly close deadline? Yes.

I once prepared a U.S. Department of Energy grant in five days almost entirely by myself. Federal energy grants are really hard! The grant guidelines are at least eighty pages long. They have a ton of required attachments and very specific requirements down to the font type.

I agreed to write the grant for a few reasons:

» **I had worked with the project manager and trusted him to be responsive and helpful.**

» **I had worked with the applicant before, and they had an exceptional staff.**

» **The project was one of the last infrastructure upgrades to help the City convert their electricity production to biomass energy.** By being able to reference these past successes, I could easily demonstrate the applicant's capacity to deliver the project on schedule and on budget.

» **A formal stakeholder group had driven development of the project for years.** This gave me the confidence in their strong working relationships to help with last minute requests like getting letters of support.

The grant was successful! I was thrilled with the outcome, but I accepted full responsibility at the beginning if it had not been. Nobody was forcing me to apply. I made the choice.

More often than not, I have been burned rushing a grant application without proper due diligence. Please let me spare you from making the same mistakes. Your success rate will be higher than average if you do nothing more than follow this rule alone: do not chase grants. Choose them wisely and intentionally.

HOW CAN I AVOID RUNNING OUT OF TIME TO PROPERLY COMPLETE A GRANT?

I avoid procrastination like it is the plague. I do not like feeling anxious or stressed, so I suppose it is just in my wiring to take care of things well ahead of a deadline. I know this is not normal! I do, however, struggle with "shiny object syndrome" and get easily distracted.

I have developed processes to account from my lack of willpower to stay focused. Students in my grant writing workshops and classes have also found these seven tips helpful for managing procrastination, and I hope you will too!

STEP 1: Develop your grant schedule working backwards from the deadline.

When I am developing a grant schedule for the kick-off meeting, I work backwards. I start by writing down the current deadline. I then step back one day, if not two, and that becomes my new deadline.

Then I step back one more day for review by whoever needs to officially approve the application. This is likely an Executive Director, the Mayor, etc.

As an aside, you do not want to skip this step, even if they are really busy. I insist the approver put in writing that they have reviewed and accept the application. You do not want the grant to be awarded and then have people coming after you saying, "You promised we would do what?!"

The day before that, I will finish assembling the attachments and the final version of the narrative. Now, I do not simply write "finish narrative".

I have multiple deadlines for different drafts of the narrative. If I want to have five different drafts of the narrative, that means about twenty days of writing (allowing for four-day writing increments).

I then factor in other deadlines, like when I will request letters of support and when I want those back. I will mark down when I want a draft budget complete and when the final budget must be done.

I will add in progress meetings with the team. These are typically quick 20-minute meetings to get everyone on the same page.

At the top of the schedule, I will note the kick-off meeting date and give myself a day or two to prepare. Remember that I need to prep the narrative skeleton and agenda before this meeting.

If you work backwards in developing your schedule and stick to it, you know exactly how much time you need to write the grant.

Tip: *The key takeaway is the more micro deadlines you have, the better. Deadlines give a sense of urgency. They light a fire underneath us.*

SAMPLE GRANT WRITING SCHEDULE

Mon	Tues	Wed	Thurs	Fri
Detailed funding guideline review. Prep narrative skeleton.	Complete meeting agenda and narrative skeleton.	Grant kick-off meeting. Write narrative section on team.	Refine grant budget. Draft a 'resolution to submit' and request for letter of support.	Supporting info from team due. Write narrative section on scope of work.
Team progress meeting. Finalize grant budget. Assign letter of support requests.	Write narrative section on project overview and benefit.	Complete draft narrative #1. Submit to 'accountability buddy' for review.	Continue editing narrative.	Continue editing narrative.
Complete draft narrative #2. Team progress meeting.	Develop map for project.	Letters of support due. Continue editing narrative.	Pass resolution to submit grant. Edit narrative.	Draft Narrative #3 due to team for review.
Finish assembling attachments. Incorporate team edits.	Submit final application to independent reviewer.	Final review and approval by the Executive Director.	Submit grant application!	(Actual) Grant Deadline

STEP 2: Develop a visual, paper-based schedule.

We all stay organized differently, but give an old-school paper schedule a try. I have found it invaluable to have a visual map that I can look at everyday next to my desk when writing a grant (or managing any deadline-driven project).

I use a large 2 ft. x 3 ft. Post-It pad to develop my schedule. Use a whiteboard if you have it. A large paper notepad from an art store. Recycled cardboard—whatever you can find!

Draw five columns for the work days of the week. Draw a row for however many weeks you are working on the project. Make the boxes large enough to fit a single regular sized Post-It.

Now take that schedule you just developed for the kick-off meeting and put it into this calendar. Be sure to block time that you will not be available when on vacation, at an event, or tied up with other work responsibilities. The point of this exercise is to be realistic with ourselves about when we are going to get work done.

When you start writing your narrative, your mind will think about everything else that needs to be done. It can be nauseating to stay focused!

Manage that noise in your head by writing a task that needs to be completed on a Post-It. Then put it directly on your calendar on the specific day that you will take care of it. You should do this as you go.

Save up those loose ends and take care of them in bulk. Once the tasks are written down and assigned a time to be completed, your mind can let them go and refocus. I personally save my loose ends for Thursday afternoons when I seem to hit a productivity lull.

STEP 3: Find someone to keep you accountable.

Did you know that we are 65% more likely to follow through with something if we tell someone we are going to do it?

Even the most motivated people need help with accountability. It can be tough sticking to self-imposed deadlines; once you let one slide, it is easy to let them all go. Then, all too quickly, the grant deadline approaches and you wonder why you allowed yourself to get so behind.

Not anymore! How do you find an accountability buddy? They are everywhere! Ideally, you find someone within your organization that can help shoulder some of the writing responsibility. You can go back and forth with different sections and push each other.

If you are carrying the weight yourself, you still must find someone that can look over your application. In the early stages, I do not ask for someone to read the narrative. It is a mess! I just need someone who is counting on me to send them my progress, so I stay accountable.

Once the narrative is at a point where it is not a waste of someone's time to read and review, I will ask my accountability buddy to provide comments.

STEP 4: Gather feedback on specific sections early and often.

Most of us are embarrassed to share our writing if it is not perfect. But this is the point of a review. Your writing can not be perfect until it is out there and getting valuable feedback.

I have no reservations about sending someone a messy draft, often asking them to look at a high-lighted section where I need their specific input. I am not wasting their time by asking them to read the full proposal. I am drawing their attention to where I need help. This approach will always propel your narrative forward faster because your editors will see something or offer extra insight that you could not have known otherwise. Collaboration is key for producing your best work.

STEP 5: Finish your first draft of the narrative as fast as possible.

I talk about this at great length in Chapter 1, but I am repeating it because this has a direct impact on you not running out of time.

Tip: *It should take you no longer than ten days to produce your first 10-18 pages of draft narrative content and preferably less!*

Most people spend too much time trying to make a certain section perfect. Worse yet, they spend most of their time at the beginning of the application, which is usually worth the least amount of points in the scoring criteria.

I like to write my narratives backwards. Start with the harder sections first. Your best arguments will develop during this time, making the overview sections much easier to write later. Remember to convey throughout the proposal the problem your project is solving and highlighting the valuable reasons why grant funding is important.

STEP 6: Have dedicated space for deep work.

Writing requires deep work. Deep work is when you are totally in the zone and focused. It is in this flow state that we produce our best, most productive product.

Talk to your boss or colleagues ahead of time to let them know when you will be writing, so they will not disturb you. Close your door if you have one. Go to the public library. Go to a coffee shop. Go to a friend's house. Go wherever you can to be in a new environment that encourages you to focus.

Post an out-of-office email reminder notifying people that you are working on a big project and unavailable. This was my out-of-office email when writing this book:

> *"Thanks for your email! I am working on a personal challenge of writing a book in five days on how to write a grant. I will not be checking my email during this time. If it is really important to reach me, you can call me. I will get back to you as soon as I can when I return!"*

Give the real reason why you are unavailable. You are working on a hard grant application. People respect your discipline to focus.

Grant writing requires going into a black hole. Some things are going to have to wait until you are done with the application. That is just the nature of what it takes to produce measurable results.

STEP 7: If you do not have the time, then do not do it.

Grants take time, and they are a lot of work. If you are not able to put forth a good product of which you can be proud, take the time you do have and channel it into something else. Perhaps pour it into further planning and developing the project or just taking care of other priorities.

If you make this choice, do not feel bad about it. We can only do one meaningful thing at a time. If you do not have the time to produce quality work, prepare yourself so you can next time.

The bottom line is that we have to take responsibility for how we use our time. We are in charge of our lives, and if there is mayhem in it, chances are good we created it. I can be especially bad about over committing and piling on projects because I want to help.

Start forming good habits now and you will be in this game for a while. Grant writing is fulfilling! You just have to learn how to beat unreliable willpower with processes for managing attention and focus.

ACTION YOU CAN TAKE RIGHT NOW

✓ Try out the paper scheduling method for your next four weeks of work.

✓ Identify at least one person that can be your accountability buddy. Ask them if they are willing to accept your grant narratives and edit them. Ask what you can edit for them.

✓ If you have a messy draft of a grant narrative and are stuck on a specific section, ask someone for help on that specific section. Do not wait until it is perfect.

✓ Start experimenting with different places you can work to be most productive.

CHAPTER 7

WHAT IF WE DO NOT HAVE ANY FUNDING FOR MATCH?

No organization is brimming with endless resources. We are all restrained in some way. Your organization is not uniquely poor. The challenge you experience in coming up with match funding is real, and it is shared by everyone else that is applying.

How do you stand apart from the pack? You get creative. And, you develop a funding strategy ahead of time.

I describe how to prepare a funding strategy in Chapter 12. In short, it is a roadmap of how you are going to get the project fully funded and implemented. The keyword in that last sentence is *fully funded.* To do that, we have to think through how we are going to leverage grants against each other as match. We also have to think of other methods for making the project budget whole.

Before I go too far, however, what is match? Match, also called cost-share, is the percentage of total project costs that need to be funded by other resources than the grant you are pursuing.

If a grant requires a 50% match and your total project cost is $200,000, you need to provide $100,000 as the applicant contribution. If the grant required 10% match, that means a $20,000 match.

Now let me give you some potential sources of local match to get you thinking creatively.

Leverage Other Grants. Leverage every grant you receive to help secure the next one. I think about it like a game of dominoes. It is much easier when a grant can leverage the next award, and the award after that. There is always a story to tell in your grant narratives that strings together the work you do.

Stack those grant pursuits as closely to each other as you can to leverage them against each other. Doing this requires up front planning. One of the reasons I prepare a funding strategy is so that I do not start pursuing anything until I know I am ready to go into campaign mode.

If you need to, start with small grants. Starting with awards between $1,000—$20,000 can help you leverage bigger $100,000+ awards. The trick, again, is to have those dominos close to each other so you leverage the small grants as match before spending them. Once funds are spent, they almost always can not count as match.

Leverage Debt. Leverage loans (often available for lower interest rates to not for profit organizations) to close the gap between total project cost and what can get grant funded. You show the funding agency that you are willing to put skin in the game by taking on some portion of the project cost.

I helped a rural community secure funding for a water treatment plant upgrade using this method. We applied for low-interest loans from the U.S. Department of Agriculture and Washington State Department of Health. The community selected the loan with more favorable terms and used that to leverage a grant award that covered over half of the project costs.

Many state and federal funding sources will award combination grant and loan packages, favoring those willing to take on project debt. For this method to work, you must have a means for repaying the loan. Documentation for loan repayment helps prove your project is viable.

Another way to leverage debt is to use it to convince the funder that your organization is ready to proceed immediately if awarded a grant. You can then use the time it takes for the funder to make an announcement (usually between 3-9 months) to pursue other grant funding sources. Here is an example of how that worked for a low-income housing development:

To secure a $550,000 grant, our team needed to convince the funding agency that we *could fund the remaining balance of the project cost. We passed a formal resolution to secure a loan if the grant was successful. While waiting for them to make an announcement, we applied for a second grant program. We leveraged our willingness to secure debt to win the first grant and leveraged the first grant to secure a second.*

In-Kind Contributions of Labor, Materials, or Services. In-kind means donated time, materials, or service. The most common source of in-kind contribution is staff time. If you are not asking to be reimbursed by grant funds to pay for your employees time, then you are contributing to the project from your organization's payroll. While you may employ this person no matter what, the project does not happen without them. Their time is a source of match.

Even in the most cash-strapped communities, I can sus out donated resources. I helped a city and tribe negotiate how they would work together to manage their road system. The city had nearly nothing to offer, but even then, we found measurable ways they could help. They agreed to provide right-of-way whenever needed and 100 gallons of diesel at the beginning of each year to be used by transportation road equipment.

We have also leveraged access to trucks, 4-wheelers, trailers, and heavy equipment as in-kind service. If we did not have those resources, we would have to pay to rent them from elsewhere. To calculate the value of these in-kind contributions, we determined the cost to buy or rent the thing that is being contributed at a fair market rate. If an organization agrees to donate materials, like gravel, get it in writing. Any in-kind contributions should be in writing and included in an attachment to the grant application.

Philanthropists and Corporate Partners. Philanthropists in your community do not usually have formal grant programs. They just support projects that speak to the things they care about. I worked on a project that secured $50,000 of funding from a philanthropist for an art initiative. He did not have any rules on how we spent the funding. He just believed that it was a good idea, and he wanted to help get the project off the ground.

Corporate partners can also be great resources. Who does your organization do business with? I had a client suggest we invite contributions for a specific project from organizations with whom the tribe worked. We secured $40,000+ from the law firm that represents them!

Corporate partners are often interested in naming rights. The CenturyLink Stadium in Seattle? You better believe they paid a hefty sum for that name! Corporate partners can also fund certain elements of a project like bleachers, or the track, or locker rooms.

Tip: *Many corporations have non-profit entities that help them facilitate community giving. The best way to learn about these is through a subscription with Instrumentl.com.*

If you approach a philanthropist or organizational partner, you need an exceptionally well-put together overview of your project. It does not need to be longer than two pages, but it should specify why you think your organizations should collaborate. If you are not graphically inclined, check out Canva. com for developing beautiful print materials.

Expand Project Scope to Include Things Already Funded. This is definitely one of my best party tricks. What other projects are happening that are already paid for? The organization you are writing the grant narrative for may already be investing their own funds into complementary projects. Or a partner organization may be already investing their own funds into an associated project. If this is happening, then you need to think about the possibility of expanding the scope of your grant narrative to be inclusive of these projects. By doing so, you can leverage those committed funds.

For example, I worked on a port expansion project where the original scope of the grant narrative focused exclusively on rebuilding the aging docks and increasing the port's capacity. The applicant had already committed funds to extend a road from the docks in the port facility to the main highway. By including the road in the grant narrative, we were able to leverage those committed funds as match.

Leverage the "Promise" of Funding *if* Awarded. Sometimes you do not have a grant in hand, or you will not find out if it was successful for several months. Writing about what you have *and will* apply for is still important for establishing urgency.

For example, you could write: "We cannot apply for funding from the Imaginary Foundation until we have secured half of the project budget. The Imaginary Foundation has expressed strong interest in our project. An award from your grant program will help us secure up to $200,000 from them."

The ultimate power play is having a letter pledging a funding agency's commitment *if remaining funds can be raised.* Even if the funder will give you the money, ask them to provide a letter with that type of wording to motivate other funders into giving.

Funders want to support projects that are destined for success. If one funder believes in you, it is much easier to get a second and third organization to believe in you as well.

Much of the success in securing grant writing has to do with psychology! Our projects are not getting funded on merit alone. We have to be convincing and persuasive to demonstrate why our project is worthy of grant funds.

Partner With Other Organizations. Partnering with other organizations can be a valuable way to achieve more. I helped the Garland Business District plan for their future. They received a $15,000 grant indirectly from the U. S. Department of Housing and Urban Development. While it was a decent award, it was not enough to get everything done they wanted.

We partnered with a local and emerging nonprofit of artists, architects and other creatives that cared about making their community better. Volunteers ended up donating over $50,000 in professional design services and capturing the community engagement process with a video[2].

---

[2]   You can watch the video here: *https://vimeo.com/146066123*

That video is still used today to engage with elected officials and funding agencies about what the community wants for the future of Garland. It is an inspirational resource that is far better than a written report.

The key takeaway is that believing match is insurmountable, is just that—a belief. It is not a truth. It is your opinion or the opinion of others. The faster you can adapt a "can do" approach, the more opportunities you will begin to see.

ACTION YOU CAN TAKE RIGHT NOW

- ✓ Make a list of potential match funding sources. What other grants can you leverage? What in-kind resources do you have?

✓ Can any parts of your project be funded by corporate partners in exchange for branding rights?

✓ What organizations can you partner with to help leverage each other's resources?

✓ Check out the Council of Development Finance Agencies website for more information on other finance tools: **www.cdfa.net**.

CHAPTER 8

HOW DO I RECEIVE GREAT LETTERS OF SUPPORT?

Want to double your narrative and not have to write it? The trick is great letters of support! Quality letters of support add heart and sincerity to your application and can nudge your application ahead of the rest.

Here is my process for securing great letters of support:

STEP 1: Develop a Contact List.

During the project planning process, list in a spreadsheet any organizations that would benefit or support your project. At minimum, your spreadsheet should include: organization name, contact name, phone, email, and columns for tracking if the letter has been sent and received. Target a list of 15-20 organizations.

Stumped on who to request a letter from? Seek support from as many disciplines and perspectives as you can. When working on brownfield grants, for instance, the team collected letters from neighborhood groups, environmental organizations, housing authorities, development organizations, professional associations, and nonprofits.

When casting a net that wide, we accomplish two things:

» We demonstrate broad support among unlikely collaborators (i.e. environmental groups and land developers); and

» We basically get 15 more pages of narrative content!

What if I am a rural community and do not have many options? That is a self-limiting belief! No matter how small or isolated your community is, there are many organizations and neighboring communities that care about your project's success. Consider these options when you feel stumped:

» State departments in health and social services, environment, or transportation.

» Cultural organizations like museums, heritage centers, or art councils.

» Neighboring communities.

» Professional associations.

» Job or skills training organizations and programs.

» Regional and state colleges and educational programs.

» Impacted businesses and nonprofit organizations.

If your community is really small and you are struggling to think of who else to collect letters of support, consider going door-to-door to collect signatures of support. If you are a nonprofit, you can get signatures or short notes from beneficiaries.

STEP 2: Prepare Your Request for Letters of Support.

It helps to provide other organizations with an outline for their letter of support. Your request should include:

» An overview of your organization and the name of the grant you are pursuing.

» A 1-2 sentence description of your project.

» A request for a letter of support from the organization you are inviting to respond.

» Instructions for the letter including:

  • Putting the letter on official organization letterhead.

  • Addressed to whoever the grant guidelines specify or your organization's highest in command.

  • Brief description of their organization as it applies to the project.

- Statement confirming support and, if applicable, information on how they will support the project during implementation.

- Statement describing any past collaboration.

» Close with a deadline on when letters are needed back (10-14 calendar days later).

I do not recommend including an example letter of support in your request. You want the author to be creative and original in writing their letter.

STEP 3: Decide During a Team Meeting Who Requests Which Letters.

Bring your draft contact list developed in Step 1 to a team meeting two to three weeks after the kick-off meeting. Brainstorm additional organizations you may not have considered and assign who will take responsibility for requesting each letter.

Getting letters of support from people in senior roles requires some tact. In many instances, the best way to get the letter is if the person highest in your organization (or as appropriate) requests it.

Generally, you want to match whoever has a personal or professional relationship within your organization with the other organization you seek a letter from. This helps pull letters through as it is easier to agree to the chore of letter writing if you are doing it for someone you respect.

After deciding who is requesting which letters, provide your team with the 'request for letter of support' developed in Step 2. Encourage them to make a personal phone call or email (definitely avoiding a mass request!).

STEP 4: Send Kind Reminders of the Deadline for Letters of Support.

Two days before the deadline for letters of support, have your team submit a gentle reminder. The good news is that if you follow the previous steps, you do not have to send many reminder emails.

Prepare to be amazed as the letters of support roll in.

Tip: *When you ask for a letter of support and do not provide a ghosted template, you receive far more compelling, heart-felt, free-form letters than you could possibly produce on your own.*

The authenticity of the letter shines through when you read it, and your grant reviewer will feel it as well. Pretty quick, you have several more pages of content that essentially serve as extra narrative!

STEP 5: Write a Ghost Letter if You Must.

Sometimes an organizational representative will ask that you 'ghost' or prepare for them a letter that only requires signature. This will happen, so be prepared to write a template letter. I still try to highlight specific areas where they can add personalized content like past collaborations. Generally though, this does not happen with more than one or two letters.

STEP 6: Save Letters Immediately in Your Project Folder.

As always, we recommend saving any attachments or emails related to your project immediately in your project folder. Nothing is worse than losing track of a letter (or worse—forgetting to include it!), because your inbox swallowed it. Track incoming letters in your spreadsheet created during Step 1.

Letters of support do not need mailed to the funding agency. You will collect them in an electronic project folder and submit them in one attachment.

STEP 7: Assemble Your Letters As An Attachment.

Once all letters have been received, consider including an attachment cover sheet that lists all organizations that provided letters. This helps the reviewer locate a specific letter and gives them a general overview of what to expect.

ACTION YOU CAN TAKE RIGHT NOW

✓ Develop a contact list of organizations
   to request letters of support.

✓ Draft a template letter for requesting
   letters of support.

PART II

Questions Grant Writing
Unicorns Ask Themselves

CHAPTER 9

HOW DO I KNOW IF I AM READY TO PURSUE GRANT FUNDING?

Early in my grant writing career, I worked with an Alaska Native village that needed funding to relocate their entire community. The community was literally falling into the Arctic Ocean from coastal erosion. The tribal administrator wanted grant funding to build a shop for the transportation equipment needed to build and maintain a winter road for relocation purposes.

I will never forget how claustrophobic I felt standing in the village. Aggressive, unforgiving waves were crashing just yards away. The land was visibly giving way to the sea. Perhaps most disturbing of all, the shoreline was dotted with abandoned homes which were tipping into the ocean.

I certainly understood *why* the project was important, and I was motivated to help. I established a grant schedule, started to write the grant narrative, and develop a project budget.

Months passed, and the project had not progressed one bit. I could not help the community achieve their goals without their participation, so I decided to call it quits.

I had wasted their time and mine because I failed to assess their readiness to pursue grant funding.

Project Planning or Bust

From experiences like this, I learned the importance of proper project planning. Ideas alone are not enough to get funded. The idea needs some meat and bones to it. It needs to have shape. It needs to have been sufficiently well planned to give the funder confidence that you will properly manage grant funds and accomplish what you say you will.

Tip: *It is tempting to jump right into the grant writing phase, but without a sufficiently planned project, you will not position yourself for success.*

Insufficiently planned projects often prove to be too much to pull off and the grant pursuit gets canceled or gets submitted in poor form.

Our projects are not perfectly planned before we start applying for a grant, but they have sufficient form to build upon! We accelerate reaching project planning milestones during the application process because grant deadlines force decision making. We always make sure, however, a minimum level of planning has been met before researching grant funding and pursuing funds.

Below are a series of questions to consider when understanding where a project sits in the planning process. Start by answering the questions listed below in a word document or text editor of your choice. (If you would like an explanation of each section, consider taking our online learn grant writing course where we break apart each section in greater detail.)

Project Overview

» **What is your project (or program)?** *We know this must seem so basic, but all too often people start pursuing funding when they are not yet clear on what they want to do. Write 1-2 paragraphs describing your project.*

» **Why is it needed?** What problem are you solving? *Funders want to solve problems that can help others. Be clear on what challenge you are addressing.*

» **Has a scope of work been developed?** *Most often, it has not been, and that is okay. Ideally, you can involve whoever will be implementing the project or program and have them prepare one to two pages that describe what will be done in detail.*

Planning & Stakeholder Engagement

» **What planning has already been completed?** *Save any information you find on past planning efforts in a project folder.*

» **How have your community and stakeholders been involved in project development?** If they are not yet engaged, how do you plan to involve them? *Funders want to see their dollars go as far as possible. Be as inclusive and collaborative as possible when developing your project. Bridge to at least one other organization.*

» **How will you measure that your program or project is successful?** *This is especially important for program based projects. Not sure how? Contact similar organizations or the grant program you are interested in and ask for a copy of their evaluation plan.*

» **From whom can you request letters of support if needed.** *You should be able to list at*

*least eight people/organizations, and prefera-
bly up to 20.*

» **If planning work remains, has your organization—or will they—set aside funding?** *This
is key because it is increasingly difficult to get
funding for planning. Organizations want to
fund projects that are ready to be implemented
now. They do not want to fund the time it takes
to plan the project.*

Technical Viability & Sustainability

» **How is the project technically viable?** *Has it
ever been done before? What unknowns could
impact the project from being successful? If it is
a capital improvement project, are project de-
signs developed?*

» **Where will your project or program be locat-
ed?** *Does your organization own the property
or the building? If so, be sure to save a copy of
the lease, property deed or any other appropriate document in your project folder. If not, who
owns it and what is your plan for using the site?*

» **How can you prove the project (and organization) will be sustainable?** *Funders want to support projects that will continue to thrive after grant funding runs out. Show your project or program will be sustained through a business plan, feasibility study, or the like. Yes these can be expensive and time consuming to develop, but they are essential to prove sustainability.*

Team

» **Who is your main point of contact for communicating with the funding agency?**

» **Who is your project manager, responsible for day to day management of the project?**

» **Who will take care of financial management of the grant?** *If you do not have an in-house grants administration person, consider contracting with an accounting firm that has grant management experience to demonstrate a strong team.*

» **Who else is on your team and what role do they play?** *Build the best team you can. If you only list 1-2 people, the project will be perceived as vulnerable if one of the key players leaves the organization.*

» **Do you need to hire any subcontractors or consultants for niche expertise?** *Do not be bashful about hiring out to third parties to assemble an unbeatable team.*

Project Cost Information

» **Has a project budget been developed?** If not, what is the plan for getting a general cost estimate? *This is a topic unto itself, but at a minimum, you need a ballpark figure of what the project will cost to do funding research. There is a big difference between funding a $15,000 program and $1.5M program!*

» **If applicable, what are your annual operations and maintenance costs?** *This is typically for capital improvement projects, but for programs it is important as well.*

» **Who prepared the cost estimate, and what are their qualifications for doing so?** *Ideally you can involve someone with professional experience. If not, consider finding someone with knowledge around project costs and have them conduct a budget review. You can then still reference their strong qualifications as contributing to the project.*

» **What sources of funding have been secured or committed, if any?** What are potential sources of match funding? *Almost all grants require some form of cost-sharing. Think through potential resources for match now.*

Readiness Assessment. Use the questions above to conduct a readiness assessment of your project to determine if it is ready to move to the next stage.

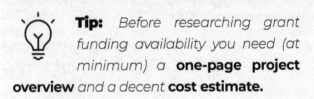

Tip: *Before researching grant funding availability you need (at minimum)* a **one-page project overview** *and a decent* **cost estimate.**

In your one-page project overview, define why your project is needed, what problem it solves, and who you are serving. You will use this one-page overview when you engage with funding agencies. You will send the prospectus ahead of time so that the funding representative can quickly learn about your project before you ask them questions about their program.

Many people skip this step, so by sending your project overview, you will already stand out from the competition by appearing professional and re-spectful of the funder's time.

Your cost estimate does not have to be perfect. A rough estimate is fine, but order of magnitude is important. There is a big difference between seeking funding for $50,000 versus $500,000. When in doubt, err on the side of caution and make your estimate a little higher.

If you are pursuing grant funding for construction, then you must also have concept drawings.

By learning how to think like a funder, you will not be surprised by the information they seek when you apply for funds.

Project planning is time consuming, and it is okay if you do not have all of the project details ready right this moment. After you have gone through the questions above and have a better understanding of where your weak points are, you will know where to focus the energies of your team to start making progress.

There is one alternative approach I want to mention here: you can research grants first and *then* develop a project to fit the grant program. This can be an effective and fun approach to finding funding and developing projects!

If you choose this route, I recommend strategically choosing grants that are not too competitive and that personally interest you. Once you have found a grant that you want to apply too, simply return to the questions above and properly plan the project.

No matter how you slice it, you cannot get out of putting in the time to plan properly! It is worth it. Well planned projects get funded!

ACTION YOU CAN TAKE RIGHT NOW

✓ Complete the questionnaire assessment for your project and identify gaps in planning.

✓ Prepare a one-page project overview.

✓ Prepare a rough cost estimate.

✓ If you want to further dive into the concepts presented here, consider taking our online learn grant writing program.

CHAPTER 10

HOW DO I PREPARE A GRANT BUDGET?

I always thought someone more qualified would prepare the grant budget and provide it to me. This rarely happened, and instead grant budgets almost always became my responsibility.

I am a "numbers person" now, but I did not feel that way most of my life. In college, I wanted to change degree programs from the business school to the engineering program. I talked to the dean of the engineering school, and he asked me what my math education had been like growing up. I told him, and I will never forget the way he laughed in my face. He said there was no possible way I could get through the engineering curriculum.

Determined to prove him wrong, I signed up for pre-calculus. I was the only senior in a class filled with freshman. The freshman had to mentor me, and I still barely got through the course. I did not become an engineer and decided to enter the engineering profession in my own way!

I tell you this story to drive home the point that I am no better at working with numbers than you may be. In fact, I am probably a lot worse!

Nonetheless, I now have no issues developing a project budget for any topic. How did I get to this point? By finding the right template.

If I had a dollar for every time I googled "grant budget template," I would have at least fifty dollars! I could never find something that worked well.

Even if you are provided a budget template from the funding agency, each one wants the information presented in a different way. Using so many different formats and ensuring that you are including everything can be confusing. This becomes especially challenging when working on a project that requires multiple grants.

Then I prepared a beast of a federal grant, and they provided a beauty of a budget template. I loved this thing, so much so that I duplicated the template for use on other projects.

In appreciation that you have hung with me this far, I am going to give you this project budget template for free. Go to **www.learngrantwriting.org/free-grant-writing-resources** to download it.

Really, go download this template right now because it is the only way you are going to follow along for the rest of this chapter. Once you have your budget template opened, start by looking at the tabs along the bottom of the spreadsheet.

Go to the tab labeled "Instructions and Summary." The cells that are light blue will automatically populate.

The information produced from this budget is designed to mirror the standard federal grant form called the SF-424A. Whether or not you are preparing a federal grant does not really matter because this is a great format to use no matter what project you have.

This budget template is my home base for every project I do; now it can be yours too.

Funding agencies often require their own budget formatting. To keep your costs straight, it is good to have one *untouched* budget in a standardized format to consistently reference.

Personnel. The tab labeled "Personnel" at the bottom of the spreadsheet means costs for employees to complete the project. We do not include subcontractors or anyone that you would be paying that is outside of your organization. Those costs go under the "Contractual" tab.

It is best not to write a specific person's name, as they could leave the organization. It is better to write the position title. Then, estimate how many hours that person will spend on the project.

This can feel complicated. I make sense of it by calculating hours per week. That is manageable to think about. Let us say it takes two hours per week on average. Then I multiply that by the number of weeks the project will take to complete. If the project takes a year, I would multiply two labor hours by 52 weeks, for a total estimate of 104 hours.

The hourly rate is the actual pay rate for that position. You can usually get this number from your organization's bookkeeper or accountant.

Fringe. The next tab, labeled **"Fringe",** are the extra benefits that supplement an employee's salary. It typically includes health insurance, subsidized meals, retirement savings, etc. Fringe is generally 10-30% of the value of one's hourly or salary rate.

You will need to get your organization's fringe percentage from your accounting staff. Usually, you can apply the same percentage across all personnel. Sometimes, more junior employees will have lower benefit percentages than senior staff, but this depends on your organization.

Travel. In the "Travel" tab, we calculate all travel that is necessary for performance of the project. It is best to estimate your costs based on rates provided by the U.S. General Services Administration (GSA). You can find this information with an easy Google search.

If we went from Denver to a conference in San Diego, I would calculate lodging, vehicle rental, meals, and incidental expenses per rates approved by the GSA. (Incidental expenses are things like parking fees). To calculate flight costs, I look up current rates and add in a buffer because fuel costs could go up. Chances are, you are not spending this funding for at least a year, so you want to be sure to account for cost increases.

Equipment and Supplies. The "Equipment and Supplies" tab can be a little bit confusing, and the difference only matters if you are applying for a federal grant.

Equipment is tangible personal property that has a useful life of more than one year and equals or exceeds $5,000 in value. That is a mouthful—basically if it is expensive and will it last longer than a year, it is equipment. If not, it is a supply. Supplies tend to be consumed during the performance of the project. Printing paper is an example of a supply.

Be sure to get quotes from vendors to back up your cost estimate. I save the quotes in my project folder but do not usually attach them to the grant application. I generally add 2-5% to the total quote to account for inflation and unexpected price increases.

Contractual. The "Contractual" tab is the costs that are related to expenses for sub-recipients, vendors, or contractors. Always save these cost estimates in your project folder in case you need to provide proof.

Construction. As the name implies, this is only relevant to you if your project involves actual construction or renovation.

Other Direct Costs. List here anything that does not fit in other categories. I rarely use this category.

In-Direct Costs. In-direct costs can be a confusing concept. They are the costs associated with doing business that can not be directly attributed to a certain project. For instance, the lights have to be on in your office, but we can not parse out what percent of your monthly electric bill is tied to each project or program.

If your organization wants to be reimbursed for indirect costs, they likely already have a predetermined overhead rate. What this means is that when you receive a grant, a portion of it goes directly to your organization for overhead expenses.

If you have a $100,000 budget and a 34% indirect rate, $34,000 goes to your organization, and it cannot be used for other project expenses. Indirect costs can add up, and some organizations elect not to use them. It will just depend on your organization and what the funding agency allows. Many funding agencies cap indirect rates at 20% or less.

Cost Share. Cost share is another way of saying match. This is where we list any sort of contributions to the project that will be made by the applicant or project partners for costs incurred and paid for during the project.

Pay attention because this always confuses people when developing their budgets. You cannot list something in the cost share tab and not also list it in any of the previous tabs. Let me give you an example here.

PROJECT BUDGET	COST SHARE
$5,000 equipment	$20,000 in-kind personnel time
$45,000 contractual labor	$5,000 cash
$50,000	**$25,000 (50%)**

In the example above, the project is said to cost $50,000 and the applicant is putting up 50% match. The problem, however, is that they have not shown the labor time in the overall project costs, so it is skewing their match percentage. Below is a correct budget:

COST	COST SHARE
$20,000 personnel	$20,000 in-kind personnel time
$5,000 equipment	$5,000 cash
$45,000 contractual	
$70,000	**$25,000 (36%)**

In this example, we made sure that the costs we are sharing are actually included in the overall project budget. By doing this, our match went from 50% to 36% (by dividing $25,000 in cost share by $70,000 in total costs). If the grant requires 50% match, we need to raise another $10,000 in cost-share funds.

With that, you can now prepare a budget! It may feel rigid and challenging the first few times, but I promise, it gets easier.

Budgeting is an iterative process. You are not going to get a finalized budget the first time you sit down to do it. In fact, it may just be an estimate until you start parsing out different expenses and gathering more information to refine your budget.

As mentioned in Chapter 1, many other elements of your application depend on having a finalized project budget. If you are looking for more help in this arena, check out our website blog and search for the keyword 'budget'. We give a number of examples on how we developed budgets from scratch, so you can see exactly how we did it.

Still overwhelmed by how to prepare a grant budget? I did not think so! You can do this!.

ACTION YOU CAN TAKE RIGHT NOW

✓ Download the free project budget spreadsheet at **www.learngrantwriting.org/free-grant-writing-resources**

✓ Prepare your first draft of the project or program budget.

✓ Request quotes from vendors and suppliers if needed.

CHAPTER 11

HOW DO I DECIDE WHICH GRANTS TO GO AFTER?

I showed you how to research grant funding, but how do you filter through those findings to select the ones worth pursuing?

There is not a right or wrong answer to this question. This is where critical thinking skills come into play. Our online grant writing course teaches you how to think through these details in a systematic way using a funding research toolkit. I have taken the main points from that resource and summarized them below.

Remember, you are going to list any and all opportunities you are considering in a Funding Matrix (available for free at **www.learngrantwriting.org/**

free-grant-writing-resources). This makes grant opportunities easy to review and compare against one another.

When determining which grants are worth your time, consider the following questions:

Why would the funding program want to support your project? You need to think through this question from the funding program's perspective. Ask yourself why your project is a good fit for their program, not why it is a good fit for you.

What percentage of applicants are typically awarded funding? This is calculated by dividing the number of successful applicants in past grant cycles by the total number of applicants who applied. If 80 applicants applied and 20 were awarded funds, we have a 25% chance of success (20/80). Often you cannot tell how many applicants applied—you can only see how many were successful. This is a good question to ask a funding agency representative.

Tip: *Seek opportunities where you have a 20% or greater chance of success.*

What was the average award size, and how much total funding will be awarded? Often, people see that you can apply for five million, so they apply for the full five million without noticing the grant agency has never made an award over two million. We want to be within a 10-15% deviation of that average award size. Review past grant award announcements and ask the funder how much funding they expect to award.

Have you read the most recent funding announcement or grant guidelines? If you are seriously considering a grant, read the funding guidelines to understand the nuances of the program. Sometimes, in the fine print you will discover important information that may influence if you want to apply or not. For example, part of your project idea may not be eligible for funding, or the grantor may have specific requirements you must fulfill before applying.

Have you discussed your project directly with the funding agency? After you have decided you are seriously interested in a grant program, you should speak with a funding agency representative. Send a one-page overview of the project to them by email so you do not spend your entire meeting talking about the idea.

In addition to any questions you may have, I have outlined below some questions that you can ask the funding agency. I recommend trying to find the answers to as many of these questions as possible using your available resources including the funding agency's website, Instrumentl, searching Google, etc.

It can be tempting to try and convince the person you speak with about why your project should get funded. The funding agency representative most likely will not personally review your proposal, or they will have a limited role in deciding if it is funded.

It is better to utilize their time for an honest conversation about whether your project and organization is actually a good fit for their funding program. If you create the space for honest feedback, it pays dividends. If they feel like you are being receptive, they will give you invaluable critical feedback on what needs done to strengthen your odds of success.

Here are some questions to consider asking a funding representative:

» **Would your organization fund a project like ours?** You believe the answer is yes if you have gotten this far, but this is a good opportunity to confirm if that is true or not from their perspective. If they say yes, ask: **What can we do to make it more appealing?**

» **Is our project eligible?** Eligibility is surprisingly more complex than you would imagine. You need to be 110% positive that your organization and project is eligible before you begin. I like to confirm eligibility with the funder and always save email documentation saying so in the project folder.

» **Why would this project *not* get funded?** This is a good thought exercise to see what your blind spots are so you can strengthen areas of weakness.

» **When is the best time to apply?** The question is not "when is the deadline?" We already know that. We want to know, strategically, when is the right time to apply for maximum likelihood of success. For example, many foundations have rolling deadlines, meaning you can submit your application whenever you are ready. If that same funder requires 50% of funds be secured before applying, that means they will be one of the last funders we pursue.

» **What must be in place to apply?** It can be tricky to figure out the small nuances of what must be done before applying. The answers are usually tucked into the corners of the funding guidelines. I worked on a park improvement project and wanted to fund it through a state recreational grant program. In the fine print, I noticed applicants must have an updated park and recreation plan. The community had allowed theirs to expire. By noticing this detail months before the grant deadline, the parks department had time to update their plan and apply later in the year.

» **Who can you partner with to make this project a success?** Often, funding is only available to certain types of organizations. Increase the number of opportunities available to you by forming partnerships with multiple organizations. A common pairing would be a local government collaborating with a nonprofit. You are highly encouraged to establish an agreement between partners to specify how you will work together. Plus, this agreement makes an excellent attachment to demonstrate your genuine commitment to collaborate. See if the funder has any specific recommendations of project partners they like.

» **What distinguishes successful applicants?** How do successful applicants present their grant proposals? Do they provide more match than required? How do they measure success?

Seek to understand the common threads that distinguish successful applicants and strive to meet or exceed those standards.

The more you practice reviewing funding opportunities and considering the aforementioned questions, the easier it gets to identify pursuits worth your time.

I usually take two passes when reviewing opportunities. As noted, I start by confirming the grant program is adequately funded, that the applicant has a 20% or greater likelihood of success, and that there is good organizational alignment.

Usually, those three questions alone can help me cull the grant opportunity list to a more manageable number worth a deep dive. As you go through this process, one of two things will happen:

1. **You find a reason the program is not a good fit and strike it from your list.** The faster you determine "keep or dump," the better.

2. **If you determine it is a good grant opportunity,** it moves to the second round of review where you confirm eligibility, discuss it with a funding representative, and decide if it is worthy of organization resources to pursue.

Once you have time to confirm the grant is worth pursuing, we then need to figure out how it fits into your overall funding strategy. In the next chapter, we explain what a funding strategy is and how to develop one.

ACTION YOU CAN TAKE RIGHT NOW

✓ Download the free grant matrix spreadsheet at

www.learngrantwriting.org/ free-grant-writing-resources

✓ Set up a free trial with Instrumentl. com to research grants. If you end up buying a subscription, use discount code mnoble0193 for $75 off.

✓ Practice your first pass on grant opportunities by assessing program fit, calculating likelihood of success, and number of grant awards to be made.

✓ For grants worthy of further evaluation, contact the funder to confirm eligibility and their interest in you applying.

CHAPTER 12

WHAT IS A FUNDING STRATEGY?

A funding strategy is a roadmap for funding your entire project. You can usually summarize everything in a two or three page memo. It is an easy document to consume, and it makes sure that everyone is on the same page.

Funding strategies will evolve as your project develops, and it is okay if it needs to change mid-way through. Ultimately, the point is that your organization is agreeing on a strategy for securing funding and adhering to a schedule to make it happen.

Here is the outline that I use in my funding strategies:

» **Summarize the project.** Describe your project, why it is needed, and what problem you are solving.

» **Specify what needs to be done before pursuing funding.** Chances are good your project has *something* that still needs to be done before applying for a grant. Specify those project planning activities here. Do you need a partnership agreement in place? Do you need a better cost estimate? Describe those action items that need your team's attention.

» **List your top funding priorities.** I will often present this information in a matrix format because it is easier to read than in paragraphs. What is the funding program? What will it fund? When should you apply, and what is your pursuit strategy?

» **Commit to a schedule.** For projects that require more than one grant, it usually takes 12-18 months to secure all funding. Include a schedule on when major action items or milestones need to be met. I include things such as when to start a specific grant, grant dead-lines, when I expect to hear back on the status of an application, etc.

Put all of that information into a document, and you have a funding strategy!

Depending on the complexity of your project or organization, it can take a few iterations to develop a refined funding strategy.

Pictured here is an early stage funding strategy. It shares my team's first round of findings for promising grant opportunities to open up discussions about where to focus our efforts. The revised funding strategy listed just four grant pursuits for the next year.

GRANT FUNDING
STRATEGY

FOR THE ALASKA OCEAN CLUSTER INITIATIVE

SENECAWORKS

FUNDING STRATEGY – Version 1

SUMMARY

Overview

There are a myriad of opportunities the Alaska Ocean Cluster (AOC) initiative can pursue to further your mission of maximizing Alaska's blue economy by uniting industry, academia, non-profit and government toward a shared blue growth strategy. Given the expansive mission and varied programs, the bulk of the opportunities identified here are targeted toward one of three areas:

- Research partnerships,
- Community level economic development, and
- The development of a blue economy coworking space.

In order to best leverage these opportunities, our recommendation is for the AOC Initiative to undergo a strategic planning process to focus on concrete opportunities for growth over the next five years. To be successful securing grant funding, it is imperative that the initiative refine its offerings and focus on the right activities for establishing sustainability and impact.

Next Steps

Step 1: Before jumping into recommendations listed on subsequent pages, we need to engage each funder by setting up a meeting or submitting a letter of inquiry to determine if it's a funding source worth pursuing.

There are a number of data points we seek that are not typically available online. We will work with you to prepare a one page whitepaper about the Alaska Ocean Cluster Initiative to share with funders ahead of your call or meeting.

We can participate in the first few calls with you to demonstrate our approach to drawing out helpful information from the funder representative. We are happy to participate in calls with federal agencies, but we have found that it is best if we are on the sidelines during conversations with private foundations.

The point of these discussions is to collect enough information to make a final determination on if the grant is worth precious organization resources to pursue. We will gauge program fit, confirm eligibility, identify areas of weakness, and calculate competitiveness.

Step 2: Based on feedback from the funders, we will revise your funding strategy to only recommend the pursuits we believe present the best opportunity for the Alaska Ocean Cluster Initiative. We will help AOC develop sub-funding plans for each priority program or project, but we recommend limiting your focus to just 1-2 areas of work.

We suggest engaging a facilitator with organizational development experience to help refine AOC focus areas. This work should be done congruently with the funding research process, so that we can confirm funding is available for prioritized focus areas.

GRANT FINDING OVERVIEW

Funding Agency	Program	Eligible Projects	Funding Available	Application Deadline	Website
The Alaska Community Foundation	ACF: Strengthening Organizations Grant	Strategic Planning	US $3,000 - US $10,000	Rolling	https://alaskacf.org/blog/grants/strengthening-orgs/

Eligible nonprofit organizations can apply to the Alaska Community Foundation for grants to build the capacity of their organizations. Grant awards will support nonprofit staff and board of directors in their efforts to access tools, develop practical skills, and cultivate support systems needed to effectively achieve the organization's mission in the areas of leadership development, organizational development, program development, collaboration and community engagement, and evaluation of effectiveness.

| Gordon and Betty Moore Foundation | Environmental Conservation: Wild Salmon Ecosystems Initiative; Oceans and Seafood Markets Initiative | General Support | Up to US $7,500,000 | Rolling | https://www.moore.org/initiative-strategy-detail?initiativeId=wild-salmon-ecosystems-initiative |

The Gordon and Betty Moore Foundation provides a variety of funding opportunities in wild salmon ecosystems, marine conservation, and sustainable seafood markets, and they have historically support fisheries initiatives in Alaska. A typical grant amount is $250,000 and they indicate willingness to provide multi-year support. The fund does not accept unsolicited proposals and requests organization provide a brief introduction and submit LOI upon request.

| National Fish and Wildlife Foundation | Fisheries Innovation Fund | Project Support (Blue Pipeline) | US $50,000 - US $100,000 | Jul 10 (Full proposal) | https://www.nfwf.org/fisheriesfund/Pages/home.aspx |

The National Fish and Wildlife Foundation will award grants to foster innovation and support effective participation of fishermen and fishing communities in the implementation of sustainable fisheries in the U.S. The Fisheries Innovation Fund was created through a partnership with the National Oceanic and Atmospheric Administration. The program seeks to support fishermen and communities as they work to meet the sustainable fisheries goals of the Magnuson-Stevens Fishery Conservation and Management Reauthorization Act of 2006, including provisions to help: rebuild overfished stocks; sustain fishermen, communities, and vibrant working waterfronts; promote safety, fishery conservation and management; and promote community and economic benefits. Pre-proposals are due in May with full proposals due in July. Full RFP is available on the website.

| Sea Pact | Sea Pact Funding Program | Program Funding (Blue Pipeline, possibly Ocean Cluster House) | US $10,000 - US $30,000 | Aug 20 (LOI due) | https://www.seapact.org/projects.html |

Sea Pact is a group of leading North American Seafood Companies dedicated to driving stewardship and continuous improvement of social, economic, and environmental responsibility throughout the global seafood supply chain. Sea Pact strives to advance environmentally sustainable fisheries and aquaculture practices and provide the building blocks for a long term and sustainable seafood industry. Projects in the following categories are encouraged to apply: gear or farm improvements; species research and data collection; research to improve farming practices; fisheries management; regional aquaculture management; technology; fishery habitat restoration ; wild stock enhancement; fisheries conservation; fisheries improvement projects; aquaculture improvement projects; and communication/education. Letter of inquiries for the next funding cycle are due August 20, 2019 with full proposals due September 20th. Application instructions can be found here.

Become A Grant Writing Unicorn • 149

SENECA**WORKS**

Funding Sources to Investigate Continued

Funding Agency	Program	Eligible Projects	Funding Available	Application Deadline	Website
North Pacific Research Board	Core Program Request for Proposals	Research Funding	US $100,000 to $850,000 depending on program.	Rolling	http://www.nprb.org/core-program/request-for-proposals/

The North Pacific Research Board (NPRB) was established by the U.S. Congress to recommend marine research to the U.S. Secretary of Commerce. Funds must be used to conduct research activities on, or relating to, fisheries and marine ecosystems in the North Pacific Ocean, Bering Sea, Aleutian Islands, Gulf of Alaska, and Arctic. NPRB prioritizes research that improves understanding of marine ecosystems and enhances effective fishery management and sustainable use of marine resources. Proposals are accepted on a rolling basis but considered twice a year at the Spring and Fall board meetings if passing the external peer review process.

| The Scherman Foundation | Rosin Fund – Environmental Program | Green Jobs | US $100,000 – US $250,000 | Jan 9, 2020 (LOI due) | http://scherman.org/programs/environment/rosin-fund/ |

The Environment Program seeks projects that re-conceptualize the challenge to spur sustainable jobs, robust economic activity, and significant social equity benefits. Specific projects may include: creation of new capital vehicles that leverage both conventional and environmental value; the engagement of new partnerships between labor, business, anti-poverty groups, and environmental groups; creation of jobs and social benefits through innovative and scalable retrofits of residential and commercial buildings; or the promotion of green industry through policies and investments. Our only hesitation with this program is how competitive it appears to be and limited annual giving.

| Rasmuson Foundation | Tier I and II Programs | Capital Project (Ocean Cluster House) | Up to US $25,000 Tier 1, up to $500,000 Tier II | Rolling | https://www.rasmuson.org/grants/ |

As a reliable local funder, the Rasmuson Foundation could be a funding partner for the Coworking House idea proposed by Jessica Edwards. It is best to start with a Tier 1 proposal (perhaps for Blue Pipeline) to build trust and rapport, before requesting a larger investment from the Tier II program.

| MJ Murdock Charitable Trust | Strategic Projects, Capital Projects, Equipment & Technology Programs | Capital Project (Blue Pipeline, Ocean Cluster House) | US $50,000 to US $500,000 | Rolling | https://murdocktrust.org/ |

The MJ Murdock Charitable Trust has a strong history of giving to organizations in Alaska. They work with nonprofits that share in their commitment to think big in solving challenging problems. They have three programs that could support AOC initiatives. Their program and staff grants can help fund both new programs and the expansion of existing programs, and may be used to cover start-up costs and/or related staff member additions. They typically fund program and staff grants on a declining basis over three years (100/57/33%). Their equipment and technology grant funds equipment and supporting technology infrastructure. The capital projects grant program funds construction, renovation, land purchase and other capital projects.

| Marisla Foundation | Environmental Grant Program - Marine Resources Conservation Area | General Support | US $20,000 to US $125,000 | Jul 15 | https://onlinefoundationsource.com/public/home/marisla |

The Environment Program concentrates on activities that promote the conservation of biological diversity and advance sustainable ecosystem management. Primary emphasis is on marine resources conservation with a geographic focus on western North America, Chile, and the Western Pacific. The Environment Program also supports the search for solutions to health and environmental threats caused by toxic chemicals. The program is well funded and we believe could be an opportunity for positioning startups as a solution for promoting ocean conservation.

| National Oceanic and Atmospheric Administration | FY 2018 – 2020 - Broad Agency Announcement (BAA) | Program Funding | Unspecified amount, likely at least $250,000 | Sep 30, 2020 | https://www.grants.gov/web/grants/view-opportunity.html?oppId=297752 |

The purpose of this program is to request applications for special projects and programs associated with NOAA's strategic plan and mission goals. The Blue Pipeline program and other AOC programmatic ideas appear to have strong alignment with their Healthy Oceans and Resilient Coastal Communities and Economies funding priorities.

Funding Strategy – Version 01

Page 5

150 • HOW TO WRITE A GRANT

Funding Agency	Program	Eligible Projects	Funding Available	Application Deadline	Website
The Oak Foundation	Environment: Marine Conservation Strategy	Advocacy and Research	More than US $25,000	Rolling	http://www.oakfnd.org/env-strategies--marine.html

In the Environment, their marine strategy for 2016 to 2020 takes a solutions-based approach to reversing the trends around overfishing, pollution and climate change to improve ocean health. It focuses on three key sectors: industrial fishing, small-scale fisheries and plastics pollution. They support organizations in the Arctic.

| Alaska Sea Grant Research Grants | Research Funding | Research | Up to US $250,000 | Feb 15 | https://alaskaseagrant.org/research/funding/#asg |

Alaska Sea Grant's mission is to enhance the sustainable use and conservation of Alaska's marine, coastal and watershed resources through research, education and extension. They support a number of formal, peer-reviewed research projects on a two-year cycle.

| USDA: National Institute of Food and Research Initiatives | Agriculture and Food Research Initiative (AFRI) - Foundational and Applied Science Program | Research and Product Commercialization Funding | Up to US $3,000,000 | Sept 26 | https://www.grants.gov/web/grants/view-opportunity.html?oppId=315674 |

The AFRI program provides funding for fundamental and applied research, education and extension projects in the food and agricultural sciences. AOC initiatives fit four of the six priority areas including: plant health and production and plant products, animal health and production and animal products, and food safety, nutrition, and health; and agriculture systems and technology. The program is well funded with approximately $182 million annually.

| USDA: National Institute of Food and Agriculture | Special Research Grants Program - Aquaculture Research | Research Funding | US $50,000 - US $300,000 | May 28 (Full proposal) | https://www.grants.gov/web/grants/view-opportunity.html?oppId=314371 |

This AFRI program funds applied aquaculture research projects to address issues related to 1) genetics of commercial aquaculture species, 2) critical disease issues impacting commercial aquaculture species, 3) design of environmentally and economically sustainable commercial aquaculture production systems, and 4) economic research for increasing commercial aquaculture profitability. We see a number of opportunities for AOC to partner with new or existing businesses to further advance R&D projects.

Making Progress

It is an iterative process to develop a funding strategy. It pays dividends to focus on the right grant opportunities. Determining which grants are right for your organization, however, often requires reflection and refinement of current operations. While seemingly burdensome at the time, this process can be a positive tool for focusing limited resources and making sure your organization is working on that which is *most* important for achieving your long-term vision.

We are thrilled to help you drive economic diversification in Alaska through a blue economy strategy. If you have any questions about this draft of the funding strategy, contact Meredith Noble at   or We are ready to help you initiate contact with funders as soon as you are ready.

A funding strategy is an organization roadmap. The roadmap is not just for you! You need buy-in from your organization. Have it reviewed by staff or colleagues, and then present it to your council, board of directors, or whoever needs to be involved.

You may also consider sharing your funding strategy with the funders you plan on applying to and asking what they think. This is strategic for two reasons: the funder sees that you are serious about funding the entire project, and it encourages them to give specific feedback on things you may not have considered.

A lot of organizations struggle with chasing grants haphazardly as funding announcements are published. A funding strategy is your best line of defense to break this cycle. If a grant is not in your funding strategy, then it does not deserve your time and resources.

We provide sample funding strategies in our online grant writing course and occasionally post them to the blog, which can be found by searching for the tag 'Funding Strategy.'

What happens if you go through this process and find out there is not enough grant funding to cover your total project cost? We will talk about what to do if this happens to you next.

ACTION YOU CAN TAKE RIGHT NOW

✓ Search our blog for sample funding strategies at www.learngrantwriting. org/blog

✓ Draft your first funding strategy and share it with others in your organization.

✓ Share your funding strategy on the LearnGrantWriting Facebook page and I'll give you direct feedback.

CHAPTER 13

WHAT IF I CANNOT FIND ENOUGH GRANT FUNDING FOR MY PROJECT?

I worked with a rural community that wanted a new administration and community building. The original cost estimate exceeded $5 million with annual operations and maintenance expenses of $50,000. Clearly, these project plans were developed when grant funding flowed more plentifully.

I asked what the community currently paid for rent and utilities. It was about $8,000 a year. Right then and there I knew there was no way we could pursue funding for this building without *right-sizing* its scope and budget. They did not have the resources to keep the building from falling into disrepair.

This meant we needed a totally new building design. Instead of getting a building with every bell and whistle desired, the facility was designed to fit what they could afford to maintain. This is how we proved to funding agencies that it was a sustainable project.

Our new budget became $1.2 million for construction, which aligned with what I thought was possible to secure in grant funding. This new building required flexibility in use of space. Instead of everyone getting their own office, it had an open layout that could be adapted when needed as a community building.

We saved $100,000+ in architecture design fees by using drawings from another community building. We needed to modify the foundation design, but otherwise it was the same.

Within a few months, my team was able to help this community get unstuck by adjusting their project scope and overall building cost. If you can not figure out how to get your project funded, consider these options:

Right-Size the project. Work with your team to determine how the project can be smaller in scope, while still meeting the needs of its users.

Phase the project. Be thoughtful about this because funding agencies do not want to fund a project that in and of itself is not complete. For example, the bowls in a skate park project are expensive. The bowl can be second phase after demonstrating how successful the skate park was from the first half of it being complete with rideable features.

Assess your match contribution. You may need to ask if your organization is contributing enough to the overall project cost. If your organization is not willing to put any skin in the game, then why should another organization do so? This can be a hard conversation to have with your boss or leadership. You have to be the first ones to support your project. You show funders that the project is a priority when using your own resources to help make it happen.

Assess your expectations. Is the amount of grant funding you seek practical? The world of grants has changed a lot. They are more complex and more competitive than years past. Is your project worthy of funding? Is it especially innovative?

You may even arrive at the answer that there are no grants available for your project. While disappointing, it is not a bad thing. You did your part to research funding availability, and now you can definitively say that the project will need to find another way to go forward.

Do not let this chapter depress you! I want you to be a successful community change-maker, and sometimes that requires you to lead difficult conversations. Dream big when you are developing your projects. Then, spend the time to right-size them so they are responsibly scoped and priced.

ACTION YOU CAN TAKE RIGHT NOW

✓ Ask if your project scope has ever been reduced. Answer if it needs further refined to be affordable and manageable.

✓ Is your organization committing enough funding as match? If not, what can be done to make this project a bigger priority for your organization?

✓ If hard conversations are required with organization leadership, write up the issues until you can refine them to a few key talking points. Prepare an agenda and set up a meeting with the project team to discuss.

CHAPTER 14

WHERE TO GO FROM HERE

Early in my grant writing career, I bought a book on the definitive guide to grant writing. It was an inch thick, perhaps more, with small font. I bet there is a lot of great information in there. Problem is, I never finished it because it was too dense and overwhelming!

When I decided to write this book, I made a pledge to not put every single thing I know about writing grants into it. It is just not the right medium for teaching everything I want you to know. We all learn better with visuals and hands on experience.

What you just read, however, are the most distilled concepts I want you to have. Much of what we just talked about is not in the nitty gritty details of grant writing, but rather about what it takes to become a respected project manager and leader.

If you do not think you are already that person, then let's get you there. We need more community change-makers now than ever.

You have taken the first step—investing in yourself with continuing education. Now, it is time to take action. Find a real project, research grant availability, identify the best opportunity, and dive into your first grant application.

If you want to take your grant writing skills to the next level, join our online program available at www.learngrantwriting.org. We provide detailed video instruction training and coaching through our private community network of grant writers. We would love to have you! As a thank you for reading this book, use discount code BOOK for 10% off the course!

I am a believer in continuous improvement. Feel free to send your questions and comments on this book to me at **info@senworks.org**. Reach out and share your successes and learnings and I will share it with our community of grant writers. Together, we will raise the bar for excellent project delivery and grant writing.

If there is one final message I have, it is this: have fun!

If you enjoy yourself, those around you will too. Grant writing does not have to be stressful or over-whelming. That is just a belief we have attached to it. Grant writing just is. How we approach it is com-pletely in our control.

You have learned harder things before. You can do this with grace and excellence. Just remember to have fun doing it! Be a grant writing unicorn!

With all of my support and enthusiasm,

—Meredith Noble

Thank you for reading my book!

I really appreciate all of your feedback, and I love hearing what you have to say. I need your input to make the next version of this book (and future books!) better. Please leave me an honest review on Amazon letting me know what you thought of the book.

Thank you so much!

Meredith

ACKNOWLEDGEMENTS

Team work makes the dream work, and this dream certainly had a team behind it.

Thank you to Holly Brooks and Rob Whitney for letting me stay at your beautiful cabin in Hope, Alaska to write the first draft of this book. Nothing is more conducive to writing than a wood stove fire and lack of internet.

Thank you Lee Brown of Geeks in the Woods for coding a custom script to transcribe audio recordings of each chapter into text files. With your innovation, I was able to write the first draft of the book in a fraction of the time it would have otherwise taken.

Thank you Gretchen Fauske, John Fogerty, Sofia Rovirosa, Kelly Willett, Dante Petri, Anna Twohig, Lucas Brown, and Conroy Whitney for editing the first draft of the book.

Thank you Elena Hartford for a professional edit of the book and Zoe Noble for incorporating them into the manuscript.

And lastly, a hearty thank you to my incredible support network of friends and family for deciding on a book title and cover and cheerleading from the sidelines to see this book to the finish line. Team work really does make the dream work.